Wales

2ND EDITION

VIEW FROM CASTELL DINAS BRAN

Authors: John Gilham
Verifier: Neil Coates

Project Management: James Harrison and Amanda Lunn
Proofreader and Indexer: Penelope Kent

For AA Publishing:
Managing Editor: David Popey
Picture Research: Liz Allen
Internal Repro and Colour Manipulation: Neil Smith
Production: Rachel Davis
Cartography provided by the Mapping Services Department of AA Publishing

Produced by AA Publishing
© AA Media Limited 2007
Reprinted 2008 and 2009
Updated and revised 2010

 Published by AA Publishing (a trading name of AA Media Limited, whose registered office is Fanum House, Basing View, Basingstoke, Hampshire RG21 4EA; registered number 06112600)

A04587   ISBNs: 978-0-7495-6889-4 and 978-0-7495-6899-3 (SS)

A CIP catalogue record for this book is available from the British Library.

Visit AA Publishing at theAA.com/shop

Printed in China by Everbest.

CAERNARFON CASTLE

CONTENTS

INTRODUCTION

There's something special about crossing the borders into Wales. Perhaps it's the way the flat fields of the English shires soar up into the Welsh hills, or the change in language on the road signs, not least 'Croeso i Gymru' – Welcome to Wales. The landscape of Wales can compete with the best of anywhere in the British Isles. Its high, jagged mountains in the north are like a child's impression of what a mountain should look like. Its quiet valleys feel remote and undiscovered. In the south, the Pembrokeshire coastline juts its rugged teeth into the foaming sea and the emphatic crests of the Brecons soar and sweep above the wooded vales. Modern Wales has a buzz but it has always kept a firm grip on its language and traditions making the country as distinct in spirit as in its landscapes; the mountains, rushing rivers and sinuous coastline.

INTRODUCTION

Borderland Wales is fertile and verdant, with rolling foothills rising to high, heather moors. Pretty villages set deep into little-known valleys like the Ceiriog and the Tanat south of Llangollen just wait to be discovered. The Conwy Valley marks the transition to the mountainous heartlands of Wales: Snowdonia. Here the great Carneddau whalebacks decline to the sea, backed up by the distinctive craggy Glyderau range and Snowdon itself. All 15 of the 3,000-foot (915m) Welsh peaks lie in a compact region between Conwy, Caernarfon and Beddgelert. Villages at the foot of the mountains like Capel Curig, Betws-y-Coed and Llanberis are dedicated to walkers and climbers. But for those who don't climb, you're never far from the yawning sands of the coast, one of those wonderful narrow-gauge steam railways or one of the great 13th-century castles built by Edward I as part of his 'iron ring' to repress the Welsh warrior princes.

In absolute contrast to Snowdonia's alpine scenery, the moorland peaks and cwms of the Elenydd region of Mid Wales are simpler in form, with wild and remote upland plateaux opening out to big, big skies.

The great flat-topped sandstone escarpments of the Brecon Beacons mark the entry to South Wales, where rural landscapes descend deep into 'the valleys'. The valleys were once the engine room of Wales. Coal, iron and steel fuelled an economy that led to massive growth in the ports of Cardiff, Swansea and Newport. After years of decline the towns and cities have been revitalised. Cardiff's vibrant new bay area with its barrage, marinas, Millennium Centre and Senedd Building brings thousands of visitors every week.

Wales meets the Atlantic Ocean at Pembrokeshire, whose spectacular coast is as rugged as anything Cornwall has to offer. It is also less busy and has fewer crowds.

UNMISSABLE ATTRACTIONS

Visit Cardiff Castle and enjoy a wealth of culture and good shopping...gaze across the Brecon Beacons...get up very high in the Snowdonia National Park...walk along the coast at Pembrokeshire or enjoy the views on the spectacular Gower Peninsula...explore the vast expanse of Fforest Fawr and the Black Mountain...discover waterfall country...visit Edward I's castles at Carnaerfon, Conwy or Laugharne...visit Machynlleth for an alternative view on modern living...take a ride on the Brecon Mountain Railway...visit the charming border town of Chepstow or walk part of Offa's Dyke...admire Thomas Telford's feat of bridge engineering across the Menai Strait or the Victorian dam of Craig Goch Reservoir, which holds back the waters of the Elan Valley...discover the mysteries of Preseli and St David's or the delightful harbour at Milford Haven.

1 Offa's Dyke
This important boundary ditch and embankment was built in the 8th century by the Mercian king Offa to divide England and Wales. It runs from Prestatyn in the north to Sedbury near Chepstow in the south.

2 Criccieth Castle
Built around 1230 for Llywelyn the Great, this superb castle stands on a headland above the lovely seaside town of Criccieth.

3 Bala
Steam engines, which once worked in the slate quarries of North Wales, are now put to use hauling passenger coaches from Llanuwchyllyn station along the lakeside to Bala.

4 Portmeirion
Welsh architect Sir Clough Williams-Ellis built this fairytale Italianate village on a peninsula on the shores of Cardigan Bay.

5 Cardiff
The city's revamped Cardiff Bay waterfront area offers plenty of shops, bars, restaurants and visitor attractions, including the Wales Millennium Centre, a showpiece arts centre for Welsh culture.

6 Menai Strait
Thomas Telford's fine suspension bridge of 1826 strides gracefully across the Menai Strait, linking ancient Anglesey with the Welsh mainland.

7 Conwy Castle
The imposing entrance to King Edward I's superb 13th-century castle dominates the town of Conwy. The castle forms part of the town's original system of defence, which includes the town walls.

Day One in Wales

For many people a weekend break or a long weekend is a popular way of spending their leisure time. These eight pages offer a loosely planned itinerary designed to ensure that you make the most of your time, whatever the weather, and see and enjoy the very best of Wales. The first day seeks out Monmouthshire's medieval history, visiting an abbey, four castles and an ancient gated bridge. It illustrates perfectly the beauty of Wales' southern border county.

Friday Night

Make your way to the border town of Chepstow. If there's time, take a walk around its pretty streets and ginnels to see the 13th-century town walls and the imposing Norman castle, which is set high on cliffs overlooking the River Wye. The Castle View Inn is the perfect choice for a relaxing start to the weekend, with fine food and accommodation.

Saturday Morning

It's well worth taking a closer look at Chepstow Castle. Now run by CADW, the castle's construction in stone began in the same year as the Battle of Hastings. The A466 to the west of the town takes the route through the beautiful Wye Valley. Visit the 12th-century Cistercian abbey at Tintern. Though roofless, the abbey is still one of the most elegant ecclesiastical buildings in Wales.

Saturday Lunch

Take a leisurely lunch at the Tintern Abbey Hotel, where you can relax in the front garden, which overlooks the abbey and the River Wye.

Saturday Afternoon

The Wye meets the Monnow at historic Monmouth, birthplace of King Henry V and Charles Rolls of Rolls-Royce fame – their statues are in Agincourt Square. Don't miss the 13th-century Monnow Bridge, the only one in Britain to have a fortified gatehouse.

Follow lanes out of town to Skenfrith, which lies among green rolling hills several miles to the northwest. The castle (free entry) is idyllically set on a green by the banks of the Monnow – wonderful for picnics. More lanes lead westwards to White Castle, a fine moated 12th-century fortress.

Now head for Llanfihangel Crucorney, before following narrow lanes that wind through the stunningly beautiful Vale of Ewyas, which cuts through the Black Mountains. Half way along is Llanthony Priory (free entry), which surprisingly has it's own pub beneath the arches.

Saturday Night

The Gospel Pass at the head of the Vale of Ewyas has superb long distance views and is an ideal place to stop and stretch your legs. Descend to the literary town of Hay-on-Wye, where Kilverts offers good, comfortable accommodation and tasty meals in the bar or restaurant.

Day Two in Wales

Our second and final day offers the chance to explore the Brecon Beacons National Park. After a relaxing start, the day gets going with a drive to Llangorse for lunch and a visit to the lake. In the afternoon there's an opportunity for a walk on a clearly defined path or you can take a ride on the Brecon Mountain Railway, one of Wales' great little steam railways.

Sunday Morning

Hay-on-Wye is a fascinating market town made famous by its secondhand and antiquarian bookshops and book festival. On Sunday morning, you'll find the town ticks over at a more leisurely pace. If the weather is fine and dry there is an easy and picturesque stroll by the river, which follows the Wye Valley Walk route westwards along the north bank. Many of the town's antiquarian bookshops open around mid-morning.

Head southwest out of the town, passing through Talgarth before taking the B4560 to Llangorse, a small village sheltering in the verdant lake-filled basin that is squeezed between the Black Mountains and the Brecon Beacons.

THE
HAY
CINEMA
BOOKSHOP

Bargain
Books

BRECON BEACONS NATIONAL PARK

Sunday Lunch

Take lunch at the Red Lion at Llangorse and if there's time drive down to the lake, which has a lovely view across to the Beacons and is good for bird-watching.

Sunday Afternoon

After heading south to the A40, head for Talybont-on-Usk, where quiet country lanes track alongside the lovely Talybont Reservoir and up to a high pass to the south of the main Brecon Beacons ridge. If it's fine and you have some walking boots, a map and three hours to spare, the clearly defined there-and-back path is well worth doing.

The lane descends into the afforested valley of the Taf Fechan, past the Pentwyn Reservoir into Pontsticill village, where a right turn leads to Pant Station on the Brecon Mountain Railway. If you didn't do the walk, there should be plenty of time for a return trip on the narrow-gauge steam railway (it takes just over an hour). There's a licensed restaurant and children's play area by the station, so this is a good spot for supper before returning home.

Anglesey & Lleyn Peninsula

The Menai Strait, between the castle-crowned towns of Beaumaris and Caernarfon, has always set Anglesey apart from its Welsh neighbours. Its dolmen-dotted interior is fringed by a coastline of steep cliffs, sandy bays and rugged seas. Over on the mainland, the narrow coastal plains rear up to the cloud-capped foothills of Snowdonia. Separated by a mere sliver of water, it's not surprising that Anglesey and the Lleyn Peninsula have much in common.

ESSENTIAL SIGHTS

Unmissable attractions

Visit Aberdaron, picture-postcard pretty and filled with whitewashed cottages, and a wide sand and pebble beach popular with watersports enthusiasts...take a walk along the coast and spot the colonies of sea birds at South Stack...gaze across the moat to Beaumaris Castle, perhaps the most beautiful of Edward I's castles, built in the late 13th century...or visit Caernarfon, the most ambitious, intended to be the seat of government and the monarch's official residence...explore the wildlife habitat at Newborough Warren, a National Nature Reserve, which covers 1,500 acres (607ha) of shifting sand dunes and forest plantations...enjoy the hydrangeas that blossom in the mild climate at Plas Newydd, beside the Menai Strait.

1

2

1 South Stack Lighthouse

Near Holyhead on Anglesey, South Stack Lighthouse Visitor Centre is reached via a flight of steps on to a suspension bridge to the island.

2 Beaumaris

One of King Edward I's most romantic-looking castles, Beaumaris was built to guard the approach to the Menai Strait and Anglesey.

3 Pwllheli
The hills of the Lleyn Peninsula rise beyond Pwllheli's elegant promenade and beach.

4 Caernarfon Castle
Imposing and stately, Caernarfon Castle is the most impressive of King Edward I's fortifications.

3

4

ABERDARON & BARDSEY ISLAND

Aberdaron is often described in tourist leaflets as being the Land's End of North Wales. This is being more than kind to the over-commercialised Land's End and unkind to Aberdaron. This old fishing village lies at the mouth of the River Daron, located at the end of the Lleyn Peninsula, and is chocolate-box pretty, with lovely whitewashed cottages gleaming against a backdrop of blue sea and golden cliffs. It is also steeped in the history of Celtic saints and pilgrims. Old Y Gegin Fawr café, in the centre of the village by the little stone bridge, dates from the 13th century, when it was used as a communal kitchen for pilgrims going to Bardsey Island.

Aberdaron's wide sand and pebble beach is popular for fishing, watersports and bathing. From here, pick up the Lleyn Coastal Path for a fabulous walk to Pen y Cil Point and views to Bardsey. St Hywyn's Church, which is located right next to the beach, is in two halves, one

Visit

NEWBOROUGH WARREN AND FOREST

Newborough Warren was created in the 13th century when storms buried farmland beneath sand dunes. Rabbits were soon to colonise the area, hence its name. To save the village of Newborough from further sand encroachment, Queen Elizabeth I made it an offence to cut down the dunes' natural vegetation, marram grass, which was used for mat-making. Later on, a pine forest was planted to offer further protection. Now a National Nature Reserve, the dunes and slacks of the area host many species of wild flowers including the marsh orchid and grass of Parnassus; there are red squirrels, too.

dating back to 1137 and the other, an extension, built around 1400. The poet R S Thomas (1913–2000), a nominee for the Nobel Prize for Literature, was the local vicar here between 1954 and 1967 and the church contains interpretations of his life and works. The exposed position of the church has resulted in damage from the sea's proximity over the years, but it is now being restored to the glory days when it would have been the last stop for those many intrepid pilgrims, before they ventured across the wild – and sometimes treacherous – waters to Bardsey Island (Ynys Enlli).

Modern day travellers can take a boat trip to Bardsey from Porth Meudwy, around the bay from Aberdaron. Visitors often get to see dolphins, porpoises and seals on their way across. They'll surely spot at least some of the island's 16,000 breeding pairs of Manx shearwaters. Bardsey, which is just over 2 miles (3km) long and rises to 548 feet (167m) at Mynydd Enlli, has been designated a National Nature Reserve. Celtic monks settled here in the 6th century but only the tower remains of the 13th-century Augustinian abbey. Many graves have been discovered on the island, giving rise to the claim that it is the resting place of 20,000 saints.

BEAUMARIS

These days the busy, non-stop A55 dual carriageway speeds most tourists on their way to Holyhead for the ferryboat crossings to both Dublin and Dun Laoghaire in Ireland. Telford's graceful suspension bridge of 1824 now carries local traffic, but it is still a superb sight, enhanced by the dramatic backdrop of Snowdonia's mountain peaks.

After the busy village of Menai Bridge you'll find the small town of Beaumaris, which is dominated by its 13th-century castle. Edward I chose the site, which he said should be called *beau marais*, which means fair marsh. Beaumaris Castle is regarded as one of the finest examples of Master James of St George's designs and wasn't finished due to lack of money and supplies. Although the walls never reached their intended height, the low-slung look is quite appealing along with the filled moat, four concentric layers of defences, private sea dock as well as the surrounding parkland.

MENAI BRIDGE

This visually appealing symmetry makes it most people's idea of a perfect castle. The town dates largely from the Victorian period, although the courthouse opposite the castle dates back to 1614. It is a major yachting centre – the Royal Anglesey Yacht Club resides here – and boat trips for fishing or sightseeing go from the pier.

Visit

THE WELSH HIGHLAND RAILWAY

Originally completed as a slate railway linking Caernarfon and Porthmadog, this ambitious line lasted only 18 years before closure in 1941. Following years of dedicated work, the line fully reopened in 2010, offering the prospect of a mouthwatering journey through the beautiful, mountainous countryside around the skirts of Snowdon to pretty Beddgelert and through the spectacular Aberglaslyn Pass. At Porthmadog it links with the Ffestiniog Railway, creating one of Europe's most extensive narrow-gauge railway systems.

CAERNARFON

Dominated by its majestic 13-towered castle, Caernarfon guards the mouth of the Afon Seiont (Saint River) and the western end of the Menai Strait. The castle is the most imposing of Edward I's 'iron ring'.

Begun in 1283 on the site of a motte and bailey castle, it would become a royal palace, designed to symbolise domination over the Welsh. It's an impressive sight with its mighty polygonal towers and powerful ramparts that are remarkably intact. It is not surprising therefore that it was chosen by the Royal Family to be the setting for Prince Charles' investiture as Prince of Wales – some 700 years after Edward's son became the first English Prince of Wales in the same place. Caernarfon Castle, now under the care of CADW, also houses the regimental Museum of the Royal Welch Fusiliers.

Powerful-looking medieval walls with imposing towered gates extend from the castle around the old town.

The narrow streets are lined with many fascinating buildings. Some, including St Mary's Church, which is built into those walls, are very old. There is an informative town trail leaflet, available from the tourist information centre, which will guide you from Castle Square through the old gates, around the old red light district of Northgate, where you'll see the 15th-century Black Boy Inn, to the castle and the old Slate Quay. The trail illustrates that this was very much a seafaring town and the Maritime Museum on Bank Quay near Victoria Dock reinforces this, with exhibits of seafaring and industry in the area.

Caernarfon's long history predates the Normans by many centuries. The Romans, under the governance of Gnaeus Julius Agricola, conquered the Ordovices (an early Welsh tribe) in AD 77 and shortly afterwards established a fort, named Segontium, to the southeast of the present town. Like many Roman forts, Segontium had

Visit

CAERNARFON AIRWORLD AVIATION MUSEUM

The Aviation Museum at Caernarfon Airport, Dinas Dinlle, tells the story of the RAF and the Mountain Rescue Service. It has plenty of combat aircraft, including the Hawker Hunter, the Vampire and Javelin, and you can even sit inside some of the cockpits. There is a museum gift shop.

defences of earth and timber, with gates and parallel streets. At the height of its strength it would have housed a thousand troops, all non-Roman citizens called cohorts. One such regiment known to have served here was called the First Cohort of Sunici, recruited from Germany. Coins discovered at archaeological digs show that the Romans occupied Segontium until about AD 394, a very long span, which indicates its strategic importance. A very fine museum here exhibits and interprets artefacts from the Roman era.

41

HOLY ISLAND

While Holyhead is the largest of all of Anglesey's towns, with a good yachting marina, a maritime museum, a beach (Penrhos) and the island's highest hill, it's a rather unattractive place, little more than a busy transit port for Ireland since the Act of Union 1801. A far better base to discover Holy Island would be Trearddur Bay on the wild southwest coast. St Brigit is said to have landed here at the end of the 5th century and the little church is dedicated to her. Here the coastline is heavily indented with rocky promontories, low cliffs and islets enclosing small sandy beaches. In the central region there is one superb sweeping sandy cove overlooked by a yacht club, the lifeboat station and the huge whitewashed Trearddur Bay Hotel, at the centre of all things local.

To the north of Trearddur the rough and rugged coastline becomes truly spectacular. The view from Ellins Tower, the RSPB information centre, to South Stack lighthouse is stunning. The cliffs of South Stack are a haven for flocks of seabirds including guillemots, skuas and gannets and the rare chough. When the wild west wind blows it's easy to see why Anglesey's perilous waters were the cause of so many terrible shipwrecks. The limestone headland of Holyhead Mountain, which lies just beyond South Stack, looks much higher than its mere 719 feet (220m) would imply. Clad with heathland it is capped by a huge Celtic fort, Cae'r y Twr, which was built on the site of a Roman watchtower.

MOELFRE & ANGLESEY'S COAST

More than any other village in Anglesey, Moelfre has a history of dramatic and daring lifeboat rescues. You can find out all about them at the Moelfre Seawatch Centre, which is sited not far from the harbour. Whitewashed fishermen's cottages are scattered on the headland overlooking a small harbour, a shingle beach and the little island, Ynys Moelfre. There are

wonderful clifftop paths to Dulas Bay, and in the opposite direction to Benllech and Red Wharf Bay.

Benllech is a modern-looking resort with a sandy beach and good facilities for families and other visitors. Just a short walk southwards on the coastal path brings you to Red Wharf Bay where there's a huge expanse of sand, tidal mud and salt marshes – the fine sands stretch for 2.5 miles (4km) to Llandonna. The bay is absolutely superb for walking and birding; you will have a very good chance of spotting redshanks, curlews, shelduck and oystercatchers. Anglesey's best pub, The Ship Inn, and the best restaurant, the Old Boat House, are here.

NEFYN & LLEYN'S COAST

Nefyn, the largest of Lleyn's northern coastal villages, has two long sandy beaches. The one below the main village is beautifully situated, sheltered by vegetated shaly cliffs and has stunning views back along the gently arcing bay to the mountains known as the Yr Eifl, (the Rivals). The view is slightly marred by a row of tatty sheds parading as beach huts. Porthdinllaen, the next cove beneath Morfa Nefyn, has the same shaly cliffs and a wonderful crescent-shaped sandy beach framed by a rocky promontory with an Iron Age

Visit

DIN LLIGWY – AN ANCIENT VILLAGE

Hidden in woodland, a mile (1.6km) or so inland from Moelfre, is a wonderfully preserved Celtic settlement. The half-acre (0.2ha) site consists of foundations of a number of buildings, with the entire area enclosed by a thick double wall, dating to the 4th century AD, during the last years of the Roman Empire. In a nearby field are the remains of a neolithic burial chamber, the Lligwy tomb. A massive capstone weighing about 25 tons covers the remains of 15 to 30 people, and pieces of grooved pottery were found here.

fort on top. The Ty Coch pub on the beach at Porthdinllaen has to be one of the best-sited pubs in Wales.

East of Nefyn the road turns inland to climb over the shoulders of Yr Eifl. Perched on the east summit of these granite mountains is Tre'r Ceiri, the 'town of giants' in legend, but in reality one of the best-preserved ancient forts in Wales. A gigantic Bronze Age burial cairn lies in the centre of an elaborate ancient settlement, where shattered stone walls enclose dozens of well-formed hut circle foundations. It's well worth taking the zig-zag roadside path through the heather to see them.

Lleyn's north coast gets more sparsely populated as you go westwards. This was largely the preserve of fishermen in days gone by – the locals still fish for crabs and lobsters – but the lonely cliffs, coves and beaches are a real haven for holiday-makers looking for a little elbow room. Porth lago has a tiny rock-bound beach – on a sunny day here you could be forgiven for thinking you were in Sardinia or a Greek island. Porth Oer, better known as Whistling Sands because the texture of the sand grains make them whistle underfoot, is a larger beach, backed by steep grassy cliffs, with safe bathing and a café.

PORTHMADOG & SOUTH LLEYN

Centred around a small harbour and the causeway William Madocks built to reclaim land on the Glaslyn Estuary, Porthmadog is the most popular holiday resort in Lleyn. Many of the visitors come to take a train ride on one of the two narrow-gauge railways, the Welsh Highland, which trundles through to Caernarfon, and the Ffestiniog, which takes a scenic route to the lovely slate town of Blaenau Ffestiniog. A short walk leads past Porthmadog's boatyards and over a heavily wooded headland to reach the sheltered and picturesque beach at Borth y Guest, a village, where life is taken at a leisurely pace. A few miles further west lies Criccieth, whose

MORFA NEFYN

castle stands on a huge rhyolite crag that juts out into Tremadog Bay. It's part of Edward I's 'iron ring' but, as there was already a Welsh castle on the spot, the English king only had to annexe and enlarge it. The twin-towered gatehouse was built by Llywelyn the Great in around 1240. The castle was left in its current ruinous state in 1404 after being captured by Welsh prince Owain Glyndwr. Despite its one-time strategic importance, Criccieth remained a small fishing port until the Victorians' craving for sun and sand saw it grow to today's proportions. There are two sand and shingle beaches either side of the castle and some excellent restaurants, cafés and bistros. Nearby Llanystumdwy was the boyhood home of one-time British Prime Minister David Lloyd George.

Pwllheli, often considered to be the capital of Lleyn, has a magnificent marina and is considered an international yachting centre. The town is good for shopping, but has a rather charmless urban sprawl, and there are better beaches elsewhere.

Ringed around a large harbour, Abersoch is a very lively resort with fine sandy beach and dunes sheltered from the Atlantic winds by the Cilan headland. This has helped attract visitors with some sort of regatta or race almost every summer weekend.

Visit

PORTMEIRION

In 1925, the Welsh architect Sir Clough Williams-Ellis began building Portmeirion as an Italianate village, on a peninsula off Tremadog Bay. He wanted to illustrate how 'the development of a naturally beautiful site need not lead to its defilement'. Pastel-coloured buildings blend perfectly with 60 acres (24ha) of subtropical gardens splashed with bright azaleas, rhododendrons and hydrangeas. The privately owned village found fame in the 1960s cult TV series *The Prisoner* starring Patrick McGoohan.

TOURIST INFORMATION CENTRES

For online information, go to
www.visitanglesey.co.uk

Caernarfon
Oriel Pendeitsh,
Castle Street.
Tel: 01286 672232

Holyhead
Stena Line,
Terminal 1, Holyhead,
Isle of Anglesey.
Tel: 01407 762622

Porthmadog
High Street.
Tel: 01766 512981

Pwllheli
Station Square.
Tel: 01758 613000

PLACES OF INTEREST

Beaumaris Castle
Castle Street.
Tel: 01248 810361;
www.beaumaris.com

Beaumaris Gaol and Courthouse
Steeple Lane.
Tel: 01248 810361

Caernarfon Airworld Aviation Museum
Caernarfon Airport,
Dinas Dinlle.
Tel: 01286 830800;
www.users.globalnet.co.uk/~airworld

Caernarfon Castle
Tel: 01286 677617;
www.caernarfon.com

Criccieth Castle
Tel: 01766 522227

Din Llugwy Ancient Village
Nr Moelfre. Free.

Ffestiniog & Welsh Highland Railways
Porthmadog.
Tel: 01766 516000;
www.welshhighlandrailway.net

Lloyd George Museum and Highgate
Llanystumdwy nr Criccieth.
Tel: 01766 522071

Plas Newydd
Llanfairpwll.
Tel: 01248 714795

Portmeirion
Tel: 01766 770000;
www.portmeirion-village.com

Seawatch
Moelfre. Tel: 01248 410277

FOR CHILDREN
Anglesey Model Village and Gardens
Newborough,
Isle of Anglesey.
Tel: 01248 440477;
www.angleseymodelvillage.co.uk
Anglesey Sea Zoo
Brynsiencyn, Menai Strait.
Tel: 01248 430411;
www.angleseyseazoo.co.uk
Foel Farm Park
Brynsiencyn, Isle of Anglesey.
Tel: 01248 430646;
www.foelfarm.co.uk
Pili Palas Butterfly
and Minibeasts Palace
Menai Bridge, Isle of Anglesey.
Tel: 01248 712474;
www.pilipalas.co.uk

SHOPPING
Market Days
Caernarfon, Sat, also Mon in summer;
Pwllheli, Wed; Porthmadog, Fri;
Holyhead, Mon; Llangefni, Thu & Sat.

PERFORMING ARTS
Galeri
Doc Victoria, Caernarfon.
Tel: 01286 685252;
www.galericaernarfon.com

SPORTS & ACTIVITIES
ANGLING
Sea Fishing
Boat trips for anglers operate from
Amlwch, Beaumaris Cemaes and
Pwllheli.
Freshwater Fishing
Cefni Reservoir, Anglesey, is good
for brown and rainbow trout.
www.llyncefni.co.uk
Llyn Maelog, Rhosneigr, Anglesey for
coarse fishing. Tel: 01407 810136
BEACHES
Aberdaron
Excellent sand and pebble beach,
popular with both bathers and surfers.
Abersoch
Sand dunes line a long sandy beach
that is shared with dinghy sailors. A
motor boat exclusion zone for bathers.
Excellent water quality.

Benllech
A blue flag beach with fine sands that are ideal for families. A choice of food and ice cream available by the beach.

Black Rock Sands, Morfa Bychan
Long, firm sandy beach that is ideal for bathing, boating, beach-cast fishing and watersports.

Borth y Guest, Porthmadog
Beautiful sandy bay.

Dinas Dinlle, nr Caernarfon
Good sandy beach popular for watersports.

Llanbedrog
National Trust owned. Long sandy beach west of Pwllheli – sheltered and beautiful.

Moelfre/Lligwy
Small beach by the harbour. Coast path leads north to the sands of Traeth Lligwy.

Nefyn
A sweeping bay with 2 miles (3km) of sand. Excellent for watersports and bathing.

Porth Dinllaen
One of the most scenic sandy beaches in Wales with a pub right on the beach.

Porth Iago
Idyllic sunbathing but very small cliff-ringed sandy cove 4 miles (6.4km) north of Aberdaron.

Porth Neigwl (Hell's Mouth)
Wild Atlantic winds and waves make this ideal for surfing. Bathing is dangerous here with strong undertows and cross-currents.

Red Wharf Bay
A sand, mud and cobble beach ideal for walks. Pub and café/restaurant.

Rhosneigr
Exposed beach excellent for watersports like windsurfing.

Trearddur Bay
Big sands and seas ideal for canoeing and surfboarding.

Whistling Sands (Porth Oer)
Splendid, isolated beach. Café in high season. National Trust (pay car park).

BOAT TRIPS

Aberdaron to Bardsey Island
Enlli Charter.
Tel: 08458 113655;
www.enllicharter.co.uk

Mordaith Llyn.
Tel: 07971 769895;
www.bardseyboattrips.com

Shearwater Coastal Cruises
Pwllheli Marina.
Tel: 01758 740899;
www.shearwatercruises.com

CYCLING

Traffic-free routes include:
Llon Las Cefni – Newborough to
Llyn Cefni, Anglesey
(12 miles/19km each way).
Llon Eifion – Caernarfon to Bryncir old
railway (12 miles/19km each way).

HORSE RIDING

Afonwen Riding Centre
Pwllheli.
Tel: 01766 810939;
www.afonfarm.co.uk

Cilan Riding Centre
Abersoch. Tel: 01758 713276;
www.abersochholidays.co.uk

Llanbedrog Riding Centre
Nr. Pwllheli. Tel: 01758 740267

Tal-y-Foel Riding Centre
Dwyran, Anglesey.
Tel: 01248 430377;
www.tal-y-foel.co.uk

WALKING

Long Distance Routes
Lleyn Coastal Path,
Anglesey Coast Path.

WATERSPORTS

Sailing Centres
Abersoch, Pwllheli, Holyhead, Red
Wharf Bay, Beaumaris, Trearddur.

FESTIVALS & EVENTS

Abersoch Jazz Festival
Jazz on the beach every Jun.
www.abersochjazzfestival.com

Amlwch Viking Festival
Re-enacts the Battle of Ynys Mon of
972, Jun (biannual).

Anglesey Walking Festival
early Jun.
Tel: 01248 725718;
www.angleseywalkingfestival.com

Criccieth Festival
Music and arts festival, Jun.

Eisteddfod Mon
Music, dance and arts – held in a
different Anglesey town each year, May.

Holyhead Maritime Festival
Music and dance on Newry Beach –
last weekend, Jul.

TEA ROOMS

Anne's Pantry
The Beach, Moelfre, Anglesey LL72 8HL
Tel: 01248 410386
www.annspantry.co.uk
Enjoy a proper, hearty Welsh breakfast, jacket potatoes or sandwiches for lunch and an evening meal in this relaxed cottage set back from the harbour. Summer visitors can enjoy dining in the pretty and lawned garden. Sunday lunch is served in winter.

Caffi Cwrt Tearoom
Y Maes, Criccieth LL52 0AG
Tea, sandwiches and home-made cakes in a charming 18th-century cottage that used to be a Court of Petty Sessions. Just off the village green, the cottage has beamed ceilings and the tea garden has a view of Criccieth Castle.

Sea View Tearooms
Borth y Gest LL49 9TR
Tel: 012144 51332
Promenade café serving sandwiches, cakes and simple hot meals, such as liver and bacon. Views from the terrace across the bay to Snowdonia.

Old Boat House
Red Wharf Bay, Pentraeth,
Gwynedd LL75 8RJ
Tel: 01248 852731
Set back from the wide sweep of Red Wharf Bay, you couldn't ask for a better view. Sandwiches and snacks are available or more substantial meals, including cannelloni, curries, lasagne and lemon chicken. Sit in the garden on fine summer days or in a cosy bistro-like restaurant.

Y Gegin Fawr
Aberdaron LL53 8BE
Tel: 01758 760359
This 14th-century building once catered for Bardsey pilgrims. Simply decorated on two floors, specialities include locally caught crab and lobster, home-made cakes and scones.

Black Boy

Northgate St, Caernarfon,
Gwynedd LL55 1RW
Tel: 01286 673604
www.black-boy-inn.com

A long-established favourite, built more
than 400 years ago using shipwreck
timbers. Sip beers from Purple Moose
and enjoy the menu of favourites and
inventive specials.

The Ship Inn

Red Wharf Bay, Anglesey LL75 8RJ
Tel: 01248 852568

Superbly located on the shore of Red
Wharf Bay, this whitewashed inn
has dark, oak beams, wooden floors
and cottage-style furniture. From
the outside tables you can munch on
gourmet sandwiches and baguettes
while looking out across the bay.
The restaurant and bar menus are
renowned for their locally caught
fresh fish.

Trearddur Bay Hotel

Lon Isallt, Anglesey LL65 2UN
Tel: 01407 860301
www.trearddurbayhotel.co.uk

This large hotel dominates the shore of
Trearddur Bay. Within the complex, the
lively Inn at the Bay offers bar meals
in an informal setting, while the Snug
is ideal for those wanting a traditional
pub atmosphere. The restaurant menu
features locally caught seafood and
Welsh beef and lamb.

Ty Coch

Porthdinllaen, Morfa Nefyn,
Pwllheli, Gwynedd LL53 6DB
Tel: 01758 720498

One of Wales' famous pubs, with great
atmosphere and a truly wonderful
beachfront position. Light meals
include ploughman's, and mussels in
garlic butter served with green salad.
Tea and coffee are available. The pub
was featured in the Demi Moore
film *Half Light*.

TRYFN, OGWEN VALLEY

Snowdonia:
Mountains & Valleys

INTRODUCTION

Snowdonia has a heart of rock
that has enticed generations of
walkers and climbers on to its
spectacular arêtes and crags,
and has provided slate for
local building. Here is the land
where the warrior princes of
Gwynedd scored great victories
in battles against the Norman
kings, who were forced to build
the formidable 'iron ring' of
coastal castles from Harlech
to Conwy.

ESSENTIAL SIGHTS

Unmissable attractions

This area has been the inspiration to poets, artists and travellers...visit Conwy and explore its superb castle...marvel at Swallow Falls at Betws-y-Coed...climb Cadair Idris, the most romantic of the Welsh peaks...explore Harlech Castle, which stands overlooking the historic town...travel on the Snowdon Mountain Railway or climb to Snowdon's summit...walk around Bala lake, the largest natural lake in Wales.

2

1 Llynnau Mymbyr
The twin lakes of Llynnau Mymbyr, near Capel Curig, are only separated in very dry summers. The waters are popular with canoeists from the nearby mountain centre.

2 Conwy
With its two barbicans, eight massive towers and great bow-shaped hall, Conwy Castle is a 'must' for visitors.

3 Beddgelert
The beautiful countryside that lies around Beddgelert in the Snowdonia National Park, offers plenty of great routes for cyclists.

4 Llanberis
The still waters of Llyn Padarn can be seen from the A4086, but it is best explored on foot on the trail around the lake.

5 Llanrwst
This attractive arched bridge, built in 1636 probably to a design by Inigo Jones, spans the River Conwy by the busy market town of Llanrwst.

6 Betws-y-Coed
Mingle with walkers and climbers at Betws-y-Coed, the most popular of Snowdonia's resorts, and don't miss the spectacular Swallow Falls.

ABERDYFI

In the most southwestern corner of the Snowdonia National Park, Aberdyfi is the finest of Merionydd's coastal resorts. The picturesque, pastel colour-washed cottages, shops and inns, and small harbour are tucked between the steep grassy slopes of the Tarren Hills and the sands of the Dyfi Estuary and Cardigan Bay. Those beaches extend northwards for almost 4 miles (6km) to Tywyn. Besides swimming, sunbathing and sandcastle building, Aberdyfi is popular for most watersports, including sailing, sail-boarding, canoeing and fishing. On most weekends yachts with a multitude of colourful sails can be seen gliding across the waves.

Inland from Aberdyfi, the Happy Valley delves into the Tarren Hills. Its river, the Afon Dyffryn-gwyn, flows from Llyn Barfog, which means the Bearded Lake. Some say that the name Barfog could relate to Barfog, the colleague of King Arthur. Tales abound about Arthur slaying the mythical beast, Afanc, here, and there's even a nearby summit rock that has the name Carn March Arthur, the cairn of Arthur's horse. Could it be more simple, and that the rushes that infest the lake's edge form the beard?

On the other side of the Happy Valley lane the Tarrens proper begin. These superb, grassy whalebacks span some 10 miles (16km) to the Dysynni Valley and offer some of the best wilderness ridge-walking in this part of Wales. Although blighted by conifer forests in places, there are many neolithic cairns and stunning views of mountain coast and estuary, especially at sunset.

BALA

Bala's jewel is its lake, Llyn Tegid, the largest natural lake in Wales. This beautiful body of water, surrounded by the Aran and Arenig Mountains, is popular for watersports, especially when strong southwesterly winds whip up the waves into white horses. The lake is popular with anglers too. Pike, perch, trout, salmon and roach are plentiful, but Llyn Tegid is most famous for the Gwyniad, which resembles a freshwater herring and is believed to have been trapped here since the last Ice Age. The town is dominated by the wide main street, whose austere architecture is camouflaged by the brightly coloured signs of cafés, gift shops and inns. Bala has religious roots, a fact reinforced by the number of chapels and the statue of Dr Lewis Edwards, founder of the Methodist College, and, opposite the White Lion, a statue of the Reverend Thomas Charles, one of the founders of the British and Foreign Bible Society.

The Bala Lake Railway, one of those splendid narrow-gauge steam railways for which the Welsh are famous, has its terminus on the south shore of the lake just over a half mile (800m) from the town. Trains run for 4.5 miles (7km) along the southern shore to Llanuwychllyn on the trackbed of the former Ruabon–Barmouth line. Close to Bala Station, the motte and bailey castle of Tomen y Mur has a long history – some historians believe that the mound dates back to Roman times. The castle was one of several captured from the Normans by the Welsh prince Llywelyn ap Iowerth (Llywelyn the Great) in 1202.

Visit

TALYLLYN RAILWAY

The narrow-gauge Talyllyn Railway opened in 1865 to carry slate from the Bryn Eglwys quarries near Abergynolwyn to the sea at Tywyn, a journey of around 7 miles (11km). The railway and the quarries closed in 1946 following a serious rock fall, but a few years later a group of enthusiasts formed the Talyllyn Railway Preservation Society (the first such organisation in the world) and took over the running of the steam railway, which still carries thousands of wide-eyed passengers through the beautiful Fathew Valley, stopping at Dolgoch Falls.

BARMOUTH

The Snowdonia National Park borders bypass Barmouth on the side of the Rhinog Mountain. The largely Victorian resort built into the rocks is a bit too much like Blackpool perhaps? When walking the promenade past the funfair and the fish-and-chip cafés visitors could be forgiven for thinking they were on the Fylde Coast, and Barmouth has been blessed with the same wonderful sands. Those who might be looking for more than a beach holiday and who choose to explore a little further, will find true beauty and majesty in the surrounding mountains and the Mawddach Estuary. The Rhinogydd range, which rises from the backyards of the resort, features some of the finest mountains in Wales.

A fascinating web of stairs and alleyways leads from the High Street up to Hen Bermo, the old town, built almost vertically and haphazardly up the cliffs. Eventually you will come to Dinas Oleu (the Fortress of Light),

Insight

THE ARAN MOUNTAINS

Towering above Bala's lake, Aran Fawddwy at 2,969 feet (905m) is Wales' highest mountain south of Snowdon. The River Dee has its birthplace in a small lake that cowers beneath the summit crags. Once locals mistakenly believed that nearby Cadair Idris was a few feet higher, and, jealous of its popularity, erected a huge cairn to redress the balance. The rocky Aran ridge includes another fine conical-shaped mountain, Aran Benllyn, which is the one that dominates Bala's lake view.

donated to the National Trust by the local Talbot family.

As there wasn't enough room to squeeze the main road from Harlech between the foothills and the sea, all roads climbed inland, over the Rhinog mountain passes. Looking down from that perch on Dinas Oleu you'll see their problem. However, in the mid-19th century a coast road was built borrowing ground

from the beach area. In 1867 the railways followed, crossing over the Mawddach Estuary on a half-mile (800m) new bridge which had a swing section to allow shipping to pass. The new breed of Victorian tourist flocked here for the sea air, the beaches and the bathing. Hotels were shoehorned into the narrow strait, built almost into the rock face. One of those visitors was William Wordsworth, who described the view across the estuary towards Cadair Idris as sublime and equal to any in Scotland.

Artists J M W Turner and Richard Wilson came to capture the changing light and renowned beauty of both estuary and mountainside.

BEDDGELERT

Beddgelert has a location to die for, tucked away near the confluence of the Glaslyn and Colwyn valleys, and beneath the lusciously wooded lower crags and bluffs of Snowdon. The centrepiece of the village is a pretty twin-arched stone bridge over the lively Glaslyn. Huddled around the bridge are the stone-built cottages, inns, craft shops and cafés. Beddgelert and the area around it once made it across to Hollywood, for many scenes from Ingrid Bergman's film, *The Inn of the Sixth Happiness*, were shot here.

Beddgelert, which means Gelert's grave, takes its name from the Celtic saint, Kelert. Some tourist literature would have you believe that Gelert was Llywelyn the Great's faithful dog, killed by his master, who mistakenly believed it had butchered his child. The myth and the building of the grave were clever ploys by David Pritchard, the first landlord of the Royal Goat Hotel, built in 1803, to bring more visitors into his new establishment.

The Sygun Copper Mines, to the north of Beddgelert, are well worth seeing. You'll travel on foot on a self-guided audio-visual tour through winding tunnels to see the veins of copper ore in the large, colourful chambers that are ornamented by a fascinating array of ferrous oxide stalactites and stalagmites.

Looking downwards onto the copper mine from Snowdon's slopes is Dinas Emrys, a rocky wooded knoll capped with the ruins of an old fort, possibly from the Iron Age and probably used in the time of Llywelyn the Great. Legends tell that it was the refuge of Arthurian magician Merlin, and of Vortigern, a 5th-century British king who was fleeing from the Danes. Access to the area is difficult, sometimes even dangerous, and is not advised.

To the south of the village the A498 Porthmadog road enters the Aberglaslyn Pass, where the flanks of Moel Hebog and the 700-foot (213m) splintered cliffs form a cavernous rocky gorge, through which the waters of the River Glaslyn transform into violent white torrents as they pound the boulders of the riverbed. There's a riverside path here for the adventurous walker, which is located close to the Welsh Highland Railway track.

BETWS-Y-COED

Betws-y-Coed, pronounced 'betoose ee koyd', is the most popular of all the Snowdonian resorts and on most days its main street, the A5, will be chock-a-block with traffic. Sheltered by enormous hillside forests and sited near to the confluences of the Conwy and two of its tributaries, the Lledr and the Llugwy, Betws-y-Coed is renowned for its waterfalls. One flows beneath the Pont-y-Pair (the bridge of the cauldron), which was built in 1468 at the heart of the village. This is always popular with sunbathers who lounge on the crags that line the banks. The Swallow Falls, best viewed from the north bank of the Llugwy, is a spectacular torrent, lying 2 miles (3km) west up the road, and well worth the hike, while the Conwy Falls are on the Penmachno end of the village, accessed from the car park of the Otter Restaurant and Café.

Each day walkers and climbers congregate before and after their mountain adventures. There are

BEDDGELERT

more gear shops than food stores. Nightlife tends to centre on the Royal Oak's Stables Bar – those wanting a seat will have to get there early especially on weekends. One of Betws-y-Coed's popular visitor attractions is the motor museum. Created from the private collection of the Houghton family, it includes several exotic and rare cars such as Bugatti, Aston Martin, Bentley and the Model T Ford.

Lead played a big part in Betws-y-Coed's early development and if you take one of the forest walks up to Llyn Parc you'll see many of the relics from the old mines. Further east is Llyn Crafnant, a beautiful mountain lake reached by narrow winding lanes from Betws or on foot along a bridleway from the next village west, Capel Curig. This place is the true gateway to the big mountains of Snowdonia and as such is considered to be the best-placed resort for weekend mountain walkers and climbers who want an early start.

BLAENAU FFESTINIOG

Arrive at Blaenau Ffestiniog on a rainy day and you'll see nothing but slate. The houses are built from it, they're roofed with it and their gardens and backyards are piled up with it – great slag heaps that disappear into the low slate-grey clouds. Slate is Blaenau's heritage and they're proud of it. The slate has been mined and quarried from the Moelwyn and Manod mountains that lie either side of the 900 foot-high (275m) valley head where the town stands. When the cloud lifts, the mountains reveal themselves to be finely sculpted with distinctive shapes – suddenly Blaenau's situation looks considerably more appealing to walkers and climbers.

This slate town has its ghostly relics. Take a look at the valley of Cwmorthin, just beyond the suburb of Tanygrisiau. A slatey track climbs beneath the Moelwyn crags past a forlorn-looking lake into a valley devastated by quarries and mines. Beyond the high-chimneyed shell of

Visit

UNDERGROUND TOURS

At the award-winning Llechwedd Slate Caverns at Blaenau Ffestiniog, visitors can take a miners' tramway into the heart of the slate mountain, where a miner guides them around spectacular 19th-century caverns of cathedral-like proportions. There's also a Deep Mine tour starting with Britain's steepest railway (1:1.8), where a 25-minute underground walk reveals the social conditions in which the miners lived as told by 'the ghost of a Victorian miner'. Above ground are re-created Victorian shops, a licensed restaurant and a pub.

the old barracks you can also see the rusting pulley wheels and the bogies of the old slate carts.

Blaenau lies at the end of the narrow-gauge Ffestiniog Railway from Porthmadog, a splendid journey around the Moelwyn and through the beautiful oak woods and along the pastures of the Ffestiniog Valley. The journey takes you past Tanygrisiau's lake and power station. These form part of a hydroelectric scheme where cheap-rate power is used to pump water up to the higher tarn, Llyn Stwlan, whose head of water is then stored until needed at peak periods.

Blaenau's smaller neighbour, Llan Ffestiniog, is a typical Welsh village with a small square and a large chapel, surrounded by verdant scenery. Roaring deep in the valley, below the village church, are the waterfalls known as Rhaeadr Cynfal, plunging into a 200 foot (60m) craggy ravine. The large rock pillar at the top of the falls, Huw Llwyd's Pulpit, was named after a 17th-century warrior and poet who resided in the village.

CONWY

Few rivers can match the Conwy for true beauty. Its source, Llyn Conwy, lies high up in moorland known as the Migneint, but soon it is tumbling down between the wooded mountainsides to Betws-y-Coed.

BLAENAU FFESTINIOG

CONWY CASTLE

Visit

CAER LLEION FORT

Conwy Mountain forms the backdrop to the town and its castle. High on the hillside are the remains of a much older civilisation, for here lies Caer Lleion fort. Evidence shows that boundary walls surround more than 50 Iron Age hut circles. The walls have almost, but not quite, crumbled to the hillside from which they came. The huts, which would have been wooden, with their roofs thatched with rushes and reeds, have not survived.

As it reaches this popular resort the river calms down, passing through lush pastures before lazily meandering across sandbars and mudflats out into the estuary between Conwy and the headland of Llandudno's Great Orme.

Conwy, the town, is one of the great treasures of Wales; a place where history parades itself around every corner. Three fine bridges, including Thomas Telford's magnificent suspension bridge of 1822 and Stephenson's tubular railway bridge, cross the estuary beneath the castle, allowing both the road and the railway into this medieval World Heritage Site.

Conwy's castle has the shape we expect in our fairy-tale castles. It dates back to 1287 when the powerful English king, Edward I, built it as part of his 'iron ring' to repress the rebellious troops of Llywelyn the Great, who had given him a great deal of trouble in his conquest of Wales. A statue of the revered Welsh prince dominates Lancaster Square.

Great town walls 6-feet (2m) thick and 35-feet (10.7m) high, with three original gates and numerous towers, still encircle the old town. The walkway along the top of the walls offers splendid over-the-rooftop views of the castle, the Conwy Estuary and the rocky knolls of Deganwy. At the wall's end, steps descend to the quayside where fishermen sort their nets and squawking seagulls watch out for the scraps. In summer there is a good selection of boat trips, some just around the estuary; others further afield to Anglesey.

Conwy has many fine old buildings. The half-timbered Aberconwy House (National Trust) has origins in the 14th century, although most of its structure belongs to around 1500. The equally impressive Plas Mawr is a large mansion, built for the Wynne family in 1576. Now in the hands of CADW, the building has fine interior plasterwork. St Mary's Church occupies a central but quiet position in the town, on the site of a Cistercian Abbey of which it was once a part; the abbey was moved by Edward I to accommodate his castle.

DINAS MAWDDWY

Dinas Mawddwy, a small village just off the main highway (A470) lies sheltered from the westerly winds by the high pass, Bwlch Oerddrws, in a sylvan hollow close to the valleys of the Cerist and the Dyfi rivers. It's a centre for walkers and climbers who flock to Cwm Cywarch where gigantic crags soar to the Aran ridges. The Dyfi Valley is simply delectable in these parts. The sleek-profiled, velvety hills with a patchwork of heather, bracken and moor grass, are mellowed by hedgerow, oak woods and whitewashed farm cottages – this is truly God's country. Indeed it used to be the stamping ground of St Tydecho, cousin of St Cadfan and one of three saints sent from Brittany in the 6th century to introduce Christianity to Wales. The ancient stone church in Llanymawddwy, a few miles upstream, is dedicated to the saint.

DOLGELLAU

Dolgellau sits snugly among pastureland that rises from the banks of the Mawddach and Wnion to the great cliffs of Cadair Idris. An impressive seven-arched bridge, Y Bont Fawr, built in 1638 but heavily

CADAIR IDRIS

modified in subsequent centuries, crosses the Wnion and leads into the market town. Narrow austere streets of stone and slate buildings lead into a large central square.

Dolgellau's origins as a village lie in the 12th century when it was attached to the Cistercian monastery at Cymer Abbey. Very little remains in the town from that period – even the old Parliament building, Cwrt Plas yn Dre, where Owain Glyndwr plotted the downfall of the English in 1398, was pulled down in 1881. The town grew during the 18th and 19th centuries from the proceeds of a large wool industry – celebrated every year in the local 'Wool Race' – and a gold rush of the same era. At its peak more than 500 men were employed in the gold and copper mines in the hills around Dolgellau.

The town had a significant Quaker community at one time. A museum in Eldon Square tells how they were persecuted. Rowland Ellis, one of their number, emigrated to Pennsylvania in 1686, where he founded the famous Bryn Mawr women's college at the University of Pennsylvania.

Come to Dolgellau early on a Sunday morning and you'll see scores of walkers, stocking up with bread, cakes and soft drinks in readiness for a trip up Cadair Idris. Steeped in Celtic legends and myths, Cadair Idris, The Seat of Idris, is the most romantic of Welsh peaks. Though not quite reaching the heights of central Snowdonia, Cadair has all the grandeur of Snowdon and a little bit more – fine crag-bound tarns, sheer rockfaces and amazing wide-sweeping views across what seems like the whole of Wales.

The mountain is set in a green, fertile landscape of oak woods, dashing streams and pretty stone cottages dotted across pastoral foothills. The main starting points for Cadair are Minffordd, which lies just north of Tal-y-llyn, and Pont Dyffrydan car park on the Old Cader Road, the start of the route known as the Pony Path.

Visit

MORFA HARLECH

This area of sand dunes, salt marshes and mudflats reaches out into Tremadog Bay. The dune system is rich in flora, including the purple-pink flowers of the pyramidal and green-winged orchids. The mudflats in the north are good for wading birds and wildfowl. Polecats have been spotted here, as have many species of butterfly, including the dark-green fritillary. As it's part of a National Nature Reserve, permits are required to stray off the beach and away from the rights of way.

HARLECH

Harlech Castle stands on a great 200 foot (61m) crag defiantly watching out over Tremadog Bay. It is one of the most dramatic castles in the United Kingdom. Although the outer walls are badly damaged, the majestic inner curtain walls and their great round corner towers are well preserved. Built for Edward I around 1280, the castle would have been protected by what were then sea cliffs (the sea has since receded to reveal coastal plain and sand dunes), while a deep moat protected the rear landward side. The castle kept the Welsh at bay until 1404 when it was taken by the Welsh leader Owain Glyndwr, who then had himself crowned here as Prince of Wales, witnessed by noblemen from Scotland, France and Spain. A long siege here during the Wars of the Roses inspired the famous Welsh marching song 'Men of Harlech'. Harlech village is quite small. The old quarter lies on the hillside by the castle, while the holiday quarter with hotels, campsites, apartments and the railway, spreads across the plains. Visitors come here for the magnificent beaches whose position, with the mountains of Snowdonia spanning the skyline across Tremadog Bay, is quite spectacular to behold. Behind the village, narrow country lanes wind through an impressive range called the Rhinog Mountains which run north to south.

ROMAN STEPS

It consists of thick beds of gritstone and shale formed in the Cambrian era – making up some of the world's oldest surface rocks. The gnarled and faulted crags are riven by deep transverse canyons that create repeated obstacles to those wanting to walk along the 'ridge'. Boulders and scree from the eroded gritstone slabs are frequently covered with knee-deep heather. Early roads, paths and tracks all ran east–west, following the natural lie of the land. The Roman Steps is one such route, climbing out of the valley of Cwm Bychan and crossing the range at the wild pass, Bwlch Tyddiad. This packhorse route was constructed in medieval times and offers a splendid and fairly easy route into these wonderful mountains.

LLANBERIS & SNOWDON

The successes and failures of Llanberis have always been linked to its mountains. From the moment in the late 18th century that they decided to quarry the slate from Elidir Fawr, Llanberis was transformed from a tiny village to the bustling lakeside town it is today. In its prime the Dinorwig Quarry employed 3,000 men, many of whom travelled from as far afield as Anglesey. When the slate quarry finally closed without warning in August 1969, mountain tourism was ready to take its place. In Victorian times, popular interest in mountains was in its infancy. Being Wales' highest peak, the tourists' attention was drawn to Snowdon and Llanberis, the village at its foot. When 19th-century traveller, George Borrow, came here he observed that people were going up or descending the mountain as far as the eye could see. The Snowdon Mountain Railway, Britain's only rack-and-pinion railway, opened in 1896. Unfortunately, the first day proved disastrous, for an out-of-control descending train derailed itself before tumbling down steep slopes. One passenger jumping from a falling carriage was killed.

LLANBERIS

Today many thousands of passengers listen to the running commentary as their steam engine travels through woodland and over a viaduct before puffing up the mountain. A sleek new summit station, visitor centre and cafeteria, Hafod Eryri, opened in 2009.

The slate industry lives on through the town's Welsh Slate Museum, which occupies the same Dinorwig site on the northeast shore of Llyn Padarn. Here you can get an insight into the miner's life and his work, watch a craftsman split the rock into fine tiles and see the largest waterwheel on mainland Britain. The museum stands on the edge of the Padarn Country Park, where footpaths climb through woodland to reveal splendid views across Llanberis, twin glacial lakes towards Snowdon.

Another narrow-gauge steam train, the Llanberis Lake Railway, chugs by the shores of Llyn Padarn, from the town centre to Penllyn at the lake's northwestern tip.

LLANRWST

Llanrwst has always flirted with tourism but has never stepped out of the shadow of neighbour Betws-y-Coed. It is claimed its three-arched bridge over the Conwy was designed by Inigo Jones, and although there's little evidence of this, it is certainly elegant. The very pretty 15th-century ivy and Virginia creeper-clad cottage of Ty Hwnt i'r Bont by the bridge is also a National Trust tea house.

Set back from the western banks of the Conwy, Gwydir Castle was for centuries the seat of the Wynn family. It dates back to Tudor times, but much of the house was rebuilt in the 19th century. The important 1640s panelled dining room has been reinstalled, following its repatriation from the New York Metropolitan Museum.

A few miles north down the Conwy Valley at Caerhun, is the site of a Roman fort, Canovium, established soon after the invasion of Wales under Gnaeus Julius Agricola between AD 75 and 77.

TOURIST INFORMATION CENTRES

For online information go to
www.visitsnowdonia.info

Bala
Pensarn Road.
Tel: 01678 521021

Barmouth
Station Road.
Tel: 01341 280787

Beddgelert (seasonal)
Canolfan Hebog.
Tel: 01766 890615

Betws-y-Coed
Royal Oak Stables.
Tel: 01690 710426

Conwy
Conwy Castle.
Tel: 01492 592248

Dolgellau
Eldon Square.
Tel: 01341 422888

Llanberis (seasonal)
41b High Street.
Tel: 01286 870765

PLACES OF INTEREST

Aberconwy House
Castle Street, Conwy.
Tel: 01492 592246
Fourteenth-century merchant's house
– one of the finest examples in Wales.

Conwy Castle
Castle Street, Conwy.
Tel: 01492 592358

**Conwy Valley
Railway Museum**
Betws-y-Coed Station Yard.
Tel: 01690 710568;
www.conwyrailwaymuseum.co.uk

Electric Mountain
Llanberis. Tel: 01286 870636;
www.fhc.co.uk
Guided tours around an underground
hydro-electric power station.

Llechwedd Slate Caverns
Blaenau Ffestiniog.
Tel: 01766 830306;
www.llechwedd-slate-caverns.co.uk
A tour of the underground world of the
slate miner.

Motor Museum
Betws-y-Coed.
Tel: 01690 710760
Exhibits include Bugatti, Aston Martin,
Bentley, Bullnose Morris and Ford T.

National Slate Museum
Dinorwig Quarry, Llanberis.
Tel: 01286 870630. Free.
www.museumwales.ac.uk

Plas Mawr
High Street, Conwy.
Tel: 01492 580167;
www.conwy.com
This is possibly the best-preserved
Elizabethan townhouse in Britain.

Quaker Heritage Centre
Sgwar Elson, Dolgellau.
Tel: 01341 424680
Tells the story of the local Quaker
community that lived here. Free.

Snowdon Mountain Railway
Llanberis. Tel: 0844 493 8120;
www.snowdonrailway.co.uk

Sygun Copper Mine
Beddgelert.
Tel: 01766 890595;
www.sygun-coppermine.co.uk
Explore a Victorian mine.

Trefriw Woollen Mills
Trefriw.
Tel: 01492 640462;
www.t-w-m.co.uk
The mill specialises in the manufacture
of Welsh double weave (tapestry)
bedspreads (carthenni) and tweeds.
Visitors can tour the mill and see goods
being made or buy from the shop. Free.

SHOPPING
Market Days
Bangor, Sun Farmers' Market; Blaenau
Ffestiniog, Tue; Barmouth, Thu and
Sun in summer; Conwy, Tue;
Llanrwst, Tue.
Trefriw Woollen Mill (see above) and
Meirion Mill at Dinas Mawddwy have a
tempting array of lovely Welsh fabrics
and tapestries.

PERFORMING ARTS
The Dragon Theatre
Jubilee Rd, Barmouth.
Tel: 01341 281697
Theatre Harlech
Harlech. Tel: 01766 780667;
www.theatrharlech.com

SPORTS & ACTIVITIES
ANGLING
Bala Lake
The lake holds large pike, also perch, eel and trout.

Crafnant Fishery
Llyn Crafnant, above Conwy Valley near Trefriw.
Tel: 01492 640818. Lake with brown and rainbow trout.

DEEP SEA FISHING
Boat trips from Barmouth.
Tel: 01341 250341

BEACHES
Aberdyfi
An extensive sandy beach, ideal for families.

Barmouth
Long sandy beach away from estuary.

Conwy
Good beach with sand dunes 1 mile (1.6km) west of the town, beyond the marina.

Fairbourne
Good sandy beach, ideal for swimming.

Harlech
A straight beach with miles of golden sand, ideal for swimming.

Tywyn
Cobbles with good sand at low tide, popular beach for families.

CYCLING
Coed y Brenin
Huge mountain biking area, with challenging routes and beginners' trails. Cycle hire at Forest Visitor Centre. Tel: 01341 440728; www.beicsbrenin.co.uk

Gwydyr Forest
Forestry, miners' tracks and byway routes at Betws-y-Coed. Cycle hire from Beics Betws. Tel: 01690 710766; www.bikewales.co.uk

SnowBikers
Guided mountain biking in Merionethshire.
Tel: 01341 430628;
www.snowbikers.com

Mawddach Trail
Multi-user track on old railway between Dolgellau and Morfa Mawddach. 9.5miles (15km).

North Wales Cyclepath
Largely traffic free for its 34 miles (54.7km) between Penmaenmawr and Talacre (nr. Prestatyn).

GOLF
Ffestiniog Golf Club
Y Cefn, Festiniog.
Tel: 01766 762637. 9 holes.
Tyddyn Mawr Golf Club
Crawia Road, Llanrug, Caernarfon.
Tel: 01286 674919. 9 holes.
PONY TREKKING
**Bwlchgwyn Farm Pony
Trekking Centre**
Fairbourne.
Tel: 01341 250107;
wwwbwlchgwynfarm.co.uk
E Prichard Pony Trekking
Felen Rhyd Fach, Maentwrog.
Tel: 01766 590231
The Trekking Centre
Abergwynant Farm, Penmaenpool,
Dolgellau. Tel: 01341 422377
Gwydyr Stables
Ty Coch Farm, Penmachno,
Near Betws-y-Coed.
Tel: 01690 760248
WALKING
The area is the best in Wales for
mountain walking. Snowdon, the
Glyderau and the Carneddau ranges
are the most popular.

WATERSPORTS
Sailing Centres
Aberdyfi
Harbourmaster.
Tel: 01654 767626
Barmouth
Harbourmaster.
Tel: 01341 280671
Conwy
Harbourmaster.
Tel: 01492 596253
White Water Rafting
National White Water Centre,
Canolfan Tryweryn,
Frongoch, Bala.
Tel: 01678 521083;
www.ukrafting.co.uk

FESTIVALS & EVENTS
Conwy River Festival
Early Aug.
Tel: 01492 596253;
www.conwyriverfestival.org
Llanberis Film Festival
Tel: 01286 871534;
www.llamff.co.uk
Early Mar, at various
venues – see website.

TEA ROOMS

Cemlyn Restaurant and Tea Shop

High Street, Harlech
LL46 2YA Tel: 01766 780425
www.cemlynrestaurant.co.uk

An award-winning tea shop serving over 20 varieties of teas, along with coffees, delicious home-made cakes and sandwiches. Try local specialities such as bara brith or fruit cake, perhaps on a sun terrace with its spectacular views of Harlech Castle, Cardigan Bay and the Snowdonian mountains.

Lyn's Café and Teagarden

Liverpool House, Church Street, Beddgelert LL55 4YA
Tel: 01766 890374

Sited by the River Colwyn in Beddgelert, the cosy café has a splendid riverside garden where you can relax with a coffee or tea. Alternatively, choose from a menu of breakfast items, snacks, light meals, clotted cream teas and evening meals. The café is licensed in the evening.

Pete's Eats

40 High Street,
Llanberis LL55 4EU
Tel: 01286 870117
www.petes-eats.co.uk

This is one of the best chippys in the world, and, if you're in a mood to be self-indulgent, look no further. It's lively with good communal spirit among the climbers and hillwalkers who mix with the locals.

Pinnacle Café

Capel Curig LL24 0EN
Tel: 01690 720201
www.pinnaclepursuits.co.uk

This lively walkers' and climbers' café serves good café grub, including all-day breakfasts, piping-hot mugs of tea and hot chocolate, jacket potatoes and delicious cakes. Ideal for big pre-walk or after-walk appetites.

The Castle Hotel
High Street, Conwy LL32 8DB
Tel: 01492 582800
www.castlewales.co.uk

A rather grand 16th-century coaching inn adorned with many antiques and some fine paintings by Victorian artist John Dawson-Watson. Dine in Shakespeare's, a brasserie-style restaurant or there's a popular bar where you can get excellent meals, but be early to grab a table.

The Groes Inn
Tyn y Groes, Conwy LL32 8TN
Tel: 01492 650545
www.groesinn.com

Dating back to 1573, the Groes Inn, which overlooks the scenic Conwy Valley, became the first licensed inn in Wales. A traditional but luxurious inn, garlanded with flowerboxes in summer, it still retains the customary beamed ceilings and log fires. Anything from a light snack to gourmet meals (with many seafood specials) can be enjoyed in the bar or restaurant. Not ideal for children.

Stables Bar, Royal Oak
Betws-y-Coed LL24 0AY
Tel: 01690 710219
www.stables-bistro.co.uk

In an extension to Betws-y-Coed's largest hotel, the Stables Bar efficiently produces tasty bar meals time after time, even though the bar is usually extremely busy. On summer evenings there's a large outside dining area where you can eat under the trees and the stars.

White Horse Inn
Capel Garmon,
Betws-y-Coed LL26 0RW
Tel: 01690 710271

A cosy 400-year-old inn with beamed ceilings, log fires and a panoramic view of the Conwy Valley and the mountains of Snowdonia. The inn is well known for its fine food, with emphasis on good local produce. It also serves a wide selection of fine wines and real ales.

LLANGOLLEN

Northeast Wales & Marches

INTRODUCTION

In the fertile landscapes of old Clwyd and the Welsh Marches the sweet shires of England have gently melded into hill country; rolling hills that rise to the high ridges of the Berwyn Mountains and the Clwydians. Hillside fortresses highlight the earlier eras of border conflict: visits to the great houses and castles of Powis, Chirk, Denbigh and Ruthin are a must.

ESSENTIAL SIGHTS

Unmissable attractions

If it's good old fashioned fun you're after rather than culture, the north coast's golden beaches at Llandudno, Rhyl and Prestatyn await your arrival...visit the great manor houses and castles of Powis, Chirk, Denbigh and Ruthin...cycle along the top of the Dee Valley and enjoy the views of verdant hills...marvel at the waterfall at Pystyll Rhaeadr or the Pontcysyllte Aqueduct, Thomas Telford's feat of engineering over the deep gorge of the River Dee...explore the Montgomeryshire hills on the Welshpool and Llanfair Light Railway...walk part – or all, if you have the time – of Offa's Dyke National Trail...discover Llanarmon Dyffryn Ceiriog, the most beautiful village in the valley...explore the elegant Victorian town of Llandudno.

5

1

1 Welshpool
The Welshpool and Llanfair Light Railway steams its way through picturesque countryside.

2 Llangollen
Thomas Telford built the Pontcysyllte Aqueduct, near Llangollen, in 1795. This inspired construction carries the great Llangollen Canal over the deep gorge of the River Dee.

3 Offa's Dyke
The Offa's Dyke National Trail winds its way through some spectacular Welsh landscape.

107

4 Llandudno
The sweeping sands of Llandudno Bay are protected by the headlands of Great Orme and Little Orme.

5 Pistyll Rhaeadr
Situated in the lovely Berwyn Mountains, Wales's highest waterfall is set in a wooded gorge.

PISTYLL RHAEADR

CEIRIOG VALLEY

'A piece of heaven that has fallen to earth' is how the last British Liberal Prime Minister, Lloyd George, described the Ceiriog Valley. The Ceiriog river, which has its birthplace deep in the heart of the Berwyn Mountains, is a tributary of the Dee. Here it flows through a pastoral countryside, dotted with small farms, that wouldn't go amiss in a Constable landscape. It's not surprising that the valley has, over the centuries, inspired three local bards: Huw Morus (1662–1709), the Reverend Robert Ellis (1812–75) and John Ceiriog Hughes (1832–87).

Glyn Ceiriog is the largest village. It expanded in the 19th century with the mining of slate and other minerals in the area. There are still remnants of a tramway that was built to convey the slate to the main line at Chirk.

Llanarmon Dyffryn Ceiriog is the most beautiful village in the valley, with a church, two old-world pubs and several whitewashed cottages clustering around a picture-postcard square. Lying by the confluence of the Ceiriog and a tributary, the Gwrachen, the village takes its name from the 5th-century missionary, St Garmon. A mound in the churchyard, known as Tomen Garmon, is a Bronze Age burial mound which is believed to be the place where the missionary once stood to preach.

Visit

ONE OF THE SEVEN WONDERS

Pistyll Rhaeadr, a remote waterfall 4 miles (6.5km) northwest of Llanrhaeadr-ym-Mochnant, is one of the Seven Wonders of Wales. George Barrow, author of *Wild Wales* (1862) saw the remote falls and described the torrent as an 'immense skein of silk'. Here the Afon Disgynfa tumbles 250 feet (76m) from the marshy wilderness of its glacial hanging valley, down tree-clad cliffs into the shadows of Tan y Pistyll, dwarfing the Welsh slate farmhouse at its foot. Most wonderfully, that farmhouse is also a licensed café.

CHIRK

The border town of Chirk perches on a hillside separating the River Dee from the Ceiriog. It is a 'must' for canal enthusiasts who can marvel at Thomas Telford's magnificent ten-arched aqueduct: this was built in 1801 to convey the canal more than 70 feet (21m) above the valley bottom. Alongside there is an even taller viaduct, built by Henry Robertson in 1840 for the railway. Both impressive structures were used to carry coal from the once thriving Flintshire coalfields.

Chirk Castle, which overlooks the town and the Ceiriog Valley, was built in 1310 by Edward I's Justice of Wales, Roger Mortimer, to replace an older, 11th-century wooden motte and bailey castle south of the town. The walls have since been decorated by scores of glazed mullioned windows, hiding the stark repressive face those powerful circular towers would have issued. The castle has been continuously inhabited since 1595 by the Myddleton family, whose heraldic icon, 'the bloody red hand' can be seen on the signs of several local hostelries.

DENBIGH

Denbighshire's medieval county town basks in the heart of the Vale of Clwyd, a wide and verdant valley dividing the rolling Clwydian Hills and the foothills of Mynydd Hiraethog's moorland.

Denbigh means 'little fortress', probably referring to the original hilltop castle belonging to the ancient Welsh princes, rather than the large Norman castle you see today. After defeating the Welsh in 1282, Edward I granted the town to Henry de Lacy, who became the first Lord of Denbigh. The castle and its town walls were completed not long afterwards. The fortress would see much action in the years that followed, culminating in a successful six-month siege of Royalist troops during the Civil War. Though the castle was to fall into decay not long afterwards, there's still much to see.

Visit

LLYN BRENIG

Llyn Brenig is a 920-acre (368ha) reservoir sited high in the wilderness of the Mynydd Hiraethog. Formed by the flooding of the Afon Fechan and Brenig valleys, the huge reservoir is very popular for fishing, sailing and walking. The Visitor Centre is full of information on the area, including its archaeological heritage. Unfortunately, some of that heritage lies beneath the water, but on the northeast shores you can discover Mesolithic camps with artefacts dating back to 5700 BC.

Sights include the gatehouse, fronted by two polygonal towers, and walls that give tremendous views of the town, valley and the Clwydian Hills. In the grounds is the 14th-century tower of the otherwise demolished St Hilary's Church and an old statue believed to represent Edward I. It takes very little imagination to conjure up images of how this powerful fortress would have looked. Beneath the castle, Denbigh has many historical corners and buildings to explore. Narrow ginnels like Back Row thread quietly through the medieval part of the town, revealing buildings from the 15th century. The town also has the remains of a 14th-century Carmelite Friary, and the walls of an unfinished 'cathedral' dreamed up by Dudley, Earl of Leicester, lover of Elizabeth I, but abandoned on his death in 1588.

Denbigh is handily placed for an exploration of the Clwydian Hills, which have long been popular with walkers who delight in the heather ridges. Moel Famau, which means 'mother mountain', is at 1,818 feet (554m) the highest of the range. Its summit monument was built in 1810 to celebrate the jubilee of King George III. The square tower and spire were wrecked by a violent gale 50 years later, and the place lay in ruins until 1970 when it was tidied up. To the west of Denbigh, and clearly in view from the ridge, are

DENBIGH

LIBRARY
MUSEUM
GALLERY

LLYFRGELL
AMGUEDDFA
ORIEL

R.G.ROYLES B.Pha

the concentric earthwork rings of Maes y Gaer, just one of many ancient fortifications on the range.

KNIGHTON & OFFA'S DYKE

Knighton, a country market town, rather affluent in its appearance, lies on the southern bank of the River Teme, surrounded by lovely, low, rounded hills. The English border, including the town's hill, Panpunton, lies on the other side of the river. Tref y Clawdd, the Welsh name for Knighton means town on the dyke, and a motte and bailey castle in the heart of town stands squarely on Offa's Dyke, an 8th-century earthwork – the only place where this happens. The main street ascends gently to a fine Victorian clock tower and then on to Market Street, with Georgian houses and businesses with traditional shopfronts, rather than the brightly coloured plastic panels of the usual high street names.

Knighton has the scant remains of two castles, the open motte at Bryn-y-Castell to the east of town, and the remains of a Norman castle, sacked by Owain Glyndwr, which can just be seen at the back of the fire station. Both are now in private ownership. The town is an excellent base for walking, and the Offa's Dyke Centre on West Street provides helpful information for visitors.

Visit

RHUDDLAN CASTLE

The 13th-century Norman castle lies just 3 miles (5km) south of the coast at Rhyl. Those who make it on foot from the resort, following the banks of the River Clwyd, will notice that the banks are uniformly straight. The need to gain access to the fortress from the sea was satisfied by canalising the river, a huge project involving 1,800 ditchers. The powerful symmetry of Rhuddlan Castle is very impressive, and Gillot's Tower, which provided access to the River Clwyd below, and the twin-towered gatehouse are the dominant features.

For centuries Welsh warlords had attacked their Anglo Saxon enemies in attempts to force them back across the Marches but, in the 8th century Offa, King of Mercia, decided to settle the disputes. He built a massive earthwork dyke running the full length of Wales, from Prestatyn to Chepstow, intended to mark out the political boundary of his kingdom, beyond which the Welsh were permitted only under strict control. The dyke in these parts is at its grandest, with clear earthwork lines straddling the moors. Today there is a well-established national trail along its length. The Glyndwr's Way, another national trail, also starts here.

Knighton is served by the Heart of Wales Railway, running from Swansea to Shrewsbury. This scenic line weaves its way through the hills and valleys of Mid Wales and is popular with walkers who want to do a linear route or those who want to see the Victorian spa towns of Builth and Llandrindod Wells.

PONTCYSYLLTE AQUEDUCT

LLANDUDNO

Llandudno is by far the most elegant of the North Wales seaside resorts. The Victorian town, whose sweeping sandy northern bay is sheltered by two great limestone promontories, Great Orme and Little Orme, also extends to a west shore looking out on to the Conwy Estuary and the mountains of Snowdonia.

The town's shopping centre is built right up to the crags of Great Orme, as is the 2,295 foot (700m) long Victorian pier, the longest and most attractive pier in Wales. Just beyond the pier visitors can take their cars up the Marine Drive toll road, which takes them on to Great Orme, where there are several well-placed car parks. The more adventurous may chose to walk to the top through a park called Happy Valley and past the ski run. Alternatively, there's a Victorian tram or a cable car.

On Great Orme there's history round every corner, with Europe's only Bronze Age copper mines that are open to the public; an Iron Age fort, caves that were inhabited in the upper Palaeolithic period, and a church, St Tudno's, dating back to the 6th century.

Colwyn Bay, situated on the other side of Little Orme, was established in the same Victorian era, but hasn't got Llandudno's elegance of architecture. The chief attraction here is the Welsh Mountain Zoo, overlooking Colwyn Bay, a conservation zoo with snow leopards and Sumatran tigers.

Beauty and elegance are diluted the further east you go, to be replaced by frivolity. Rhyl, which developed into a successful resort in Victorian days, has wall-to-wall caravan parks, a pleasure beach, plenty of kiss-me-quick hats and candy floss – just the ticket if you like that sort of thing; bedlam if you don't. The beaches are excellent and it might just be the place to keep the children happy.

Prestatyn, the last resort before the Point of Ayr and the Dee Estuary, has the hills for back up. Here the

125

Clwydians come down to the sea, as does the Offa's Dyke long distance path. In times gone by the land around here extended much further north and there are remnants of a forest, which at low tide has yielded artefacts of neolithic man.

LLANGOLLEN

This self-proclaimed gateway to Wales sits very prettily in the fertile and verdant Dee Valley, surrounded by the Llantysilio and Berwyn mountains. The river is at the heart of the town and on any fair day you'll see scores of people congregating around the Elizabethan stone bridge, one of the Seven Wonders of Wales, watching the fast waters bursting over the riverbed rocks.

The bridge was extended in 1863 for the railway line, which linked Wrexham with Barmouth. Following the railway's closure in the 1960s, a preservation society was formed and today steam trains operate 7.5 miles (12km) to Carrog. The society expects that it will eventually reopen the line to Corwen. Llangollen station is a reminder of days gone by, with its historic steam engines and rolling stock lined up on platforms that are spanned by the original Great Western Railway footbridge.

The Llangollen canal runs parallel to the railway and road. Pioneered by Thomas Telford, it provides another transport leisure link for horse-drawn narrowboats, which take visitors along the canal and over the Pontcysyllte Aqueduct, where a cast-iron trough carries the canal for 1,007 feet (300m), 120 feet (35m) above the River Dee.

Looking to the skies you can see the ruffled outlines of castle ruins perched on a limestone knoll above the town. Known as Dinas Bran, it was occupied by the Princes of Powys. A walk up the hill reveals that the ruins are quite extensive and the views up the Dee Valley are tremendous – they're far better than the famed Horseshoe Pass, a 4-mile (6km) drive away. Behind Dinas Bran

Visit

MONTGOMERY

Montgomery ticks over at an altogether more leisurely pace than Welshpool. This fine country town has an elegant red-brick town hall with a clock tower and a half-timbered 16th-century inn, the Dragon Hotel, dominated by its medieval castle, established by William I's friend, Roger de Montgomery. The huge earthworks of the Fridd Faldwyn fort were built long before the Roman Conquest. Artefacts, including neolithic tools, are now held in the National Museum in Cardiff. Montgomery is also a good starting point to see a well-preserved section of Offa's Dyke on either side of the road between Montgomery and Chirbury. You can just imagine how this impressive late 8th-century earthwork might have looked by the 20-foot (7m) deep ditches here. Montgomery's ruined castle dominates the landscape along this section of the path, drawing you back to this charming and historic town.

are the long tiered limestone cliffs of Creigiau Eglwyseg. One of the most impressive sights of the region, they stretch to a place called World's End!

Just off the A542 Horseshoe Pass road in the deep, narrow Eglwyseg Valley, lies the ruined abbey of Valle Crucis, a name that means valley of the cross. This was a reference to the cross that used to top the Pillar of Eliseg, a memorial to the 9th-century Prince of Powys. Established in 1201 by Cistercian monks from Strata Marcella near Welshpool, the abbey is sited in fertile pastures beneath a knoll delightfully named the Velvet Hill.

WELSHPOOL

Set amid Montgomeryshire's rolling verdant hills and wide valley of the River Severn, Welshpool, Y Trallwng to give it its Welsh name, has over the centuries become a prosperous and bustling market town. Until 1835 it was known as Pool; some of the old mileposts still refer to it in that way. The Welsh translation was added to distinguish the place from Poole in Dorset. It was the Severn that brought trade to the town, for it was navigable by boat. The Montgomery Canal came to the town in 1797, part of a 33-mile (53km) system from Welsh Frankton in Shropshire to Newtown in Powys. Today's visitor can find out much more at the Powysland Museum and Montgomery Canal Centre, where there is a V-shaped basin used as a winding point and as a base for the Montgomery Canal Cruises.

The pride of Welshpool's town centre is its High Street, a thoroughfare of fine architecture, much dating from the Georgian era, like the Royal Oak Hotel, but many much older half-timbered buildings, such as the Talbot Hotel and numbers 8–11 belong to the 16th century. A building with a more dubious past is the Cockpit on New Street, which would have been the popular venue for cockfights until the ban of 1849. Almost every tourist who comes to Welshpool comes to see Powis Castle, which was built for the warring Princes of Powys in around 1200. A long drive from Park Lane off the High Street leads through the fine estate's parklands, past mature oaks and grazing deer to reach the castle. Because of its continuous occupation since 1578, when the ownership passed to the Herbert family, the old fortress has become more of a mansion, with castellated ramparts, tall chimneys, rows of fine leaded windows and fine 17th-century balustraded terraces overlooking manicured lawns and neatly clipped yews. Lead statues of a shepherd and shepherdess survive and keep watch over the many shrubs and perennial borders.

For those visitors wanting to explore the Montgomeryshire hills even further in a nostalgic form of transport, the Welshpool and Llanfair Light Railway can take you on an interesting journey through the picturesque and verdant Banwy Valley to Llanfair Caereinion – be sure to take your camera.

TOURIST INFORMATION CENTRES

Knighton
Offa's Dyke Centre.
Tel: 01547 529424

Llandudno
Library.
Tel: 01492 577577

Llangollen
Castle Street.
Tel: 01978 860828

Welshpool
Vicarage Gardens.
Tel: 01938 552043

PLACES OF INTEREST

Chirk Castle
Chirk, Near Wrexham.
Tel: 01691 777701

Great Orme Mines
Great Orme, Llandudno.
Tel: 01492 870447;
www.greatormemines.info
Fascinating Bronze Age copper mines.

Llangollen Steam Railway
Abbey Road,
Llangollen.
Tel: 01978 860951 (timetable);
www.llangollen-railway.co.uk

Llangollen Wharf
Llangollen.
Tel: 01978 860702;
www.horsedrawnboats.co.uk
Narrowboat trips over the great
Telford aqueduct.

Powis Castle
Welshpool.
Tel: 01938 551944
Medieval castle with a fine
collection of paintings.

**Powysland Museum
and Canal Centre**
The museum illustrates the history of
Montgomeryshire, including its canal.

Rhyl Sky Tower
Rhyl Promenade.
A 240-foot (73m) modern tower whose
observation car rotates to give birds'
eye views of the North Wales coast.

Spaceguard Centre
Knighton.
Tel: 01547 520247;
www.spaceguarduk.com
Join the search for asteroids
and comets.

Welshpool and
Llanfair Light Railway
The Station, Llanfair Caereinion.
Tel: 01938 810441;
www.wllr.org.uk
Narrow-gauge steam railway between
Welshpool and Llanfair Caereinion.

FOR CHILDREN
Alice in Wonderland Centre
Llandudno.
Tel: 01492 860082;
www.wonderland.co.uk
Alice in Wonderland and its connections
to Llandudno.
Harlequin Puppet Theatre
Rhos-on-Sea Promenade, Colwyn Bay.
Tel: 01492 548166
Britain's only permanent marionette
theatre.
Rhyl Sun Centre
East Parade, Rhyl.
Tel: 01745 344433
An indoor tropical water park.
SeaQuarium
Promenade, Rhyl.
Tel: 01745 344660;
www.seaquarium.co.uk

SHOPPING
Market Days
Colwyn Bay, Tue and Sat – farmers'
market, Thu;
Denbigh, Wed;
Knighton, Thu; Llangollen, Tue;
Prestatyn, Tue, Fri, Sat; Ruthin, Thu;
Welshpool, Mon; Wrexham, Mon.

PERFORMING ARTS
Clwyd Theatre
Mold. Tel: 0845 330 3565
Theatr Colwyn
Abergele Road, Colwyn Bay.
Tel: 01492 532668
Venue Cymru
Promenade, Llandudno.
Tel: 01492 872000;
www.venuecymru.co.uk

SPORTS & ACTIVITIES
ANGLING
Fly Fishing
Llyn Brenig.
Fly fishing for rainbow trout. Permits
from Llyn Brenig Visitor Centre.
Tel: 01490 420463
Day permits from machines.

131

BEACHES

Abergele

A good beach popular with windsurfers and canoeists. Good car parking.

Colwyn Bay

A lively pier and a good arcing sandy beach sheltered by the Little Orme.

Llandudno

Two excellent sandy beaches either side of the Great Orme. The West Beach has a pier and many activities like Punch and Judy shows.

Prestatyn

4 miles (6.5km) of sand, very popular with families.

Rhyl

3 miles (5km) of sand, good for families.

CYCLING

For challenging routes on the Clwydian range of grassy hills. www.rridetheclwyds.com

Llandegla Forest & Llyn Brenig

Forest and waterside trails
Bike hire:
Tel: 01978 751656;
www.oneplanetadventure.com

GOLF

Chirk Golf Club

Chirk, Nr Wrexham.
Tel: 01691 774407. 18 holes.

Knighton Golf Club

Ffrydd Wood, Knighton.
Tel: 01547 528646. 9 holes.

Llanymynech Golf Club

Pant, Nr Oswestry.
Tel: 01691 830983. 18 holes.

Old Colwyn Golf Club

Woodland Avenue, Old Colwyn.
Tel: 01492 515581
9 holes.

Rhos-on-Sea Golf Club

Glan-y-mor Road, Penrhyn Bay,
Llandudno.
Tel: 01492 549641.
18 holes.

HORSE RIDING

Bridlewood Riding Centre

Prestatyn.
Tel: 01745 888922;
www.bridlewood.co.uk

Ceiriog Valley

Pont-y-Meibion, Glyn Ceiriog,
Llangollen.
Tel: 01691 718686

Mill Pony Trekking
Bwlch Y Ffridd, Newtown, Powys.
Tel: 01686 688440
Springhill Farm
Riding Stables
Selattyn, Oswestry.
Tel: 01691 718406;
www.atspringhill.co.uk
SKIING
Llandudno Ski and
Snowboard Centre
Wyddfyd, Great Orme, Llandudno.
Tel: 01492 874707;
www.llandudnoskislope.co.uk
WALKING
Long Distance Routes
Offa's Dyke Path (Chepstow
to Prestatyn).
Good walking opportunities on
Clwydian Hills, Loggerheads Country
Park and the Berwyn Hills.
WATERSPORTS
Canoeing and Rafting
JJ Canoeing and Rafting,
Mile End Mill, Berwyn Road,
Llangollen. Tel: 01978 860763;
www.jjraftcanoe.com
Llangollen activity centre.

FESTIVALS & EVENTS
Llangollen International Eisteddfod
Tel: 01978 862000
Music dance and culture, early Jul.
North Wales International Music
Festival
St Asaph, Sep.
Tel: 01745 584508;
www.northwalesmusicfestival.co.uk
Ruthin Festival
Tel: 01824 703832
Music festival, Jun/Jul.

133

TEA ROOMS

Badgers Café and Patisserie
The Victoria Centre, Mostyn Street,
Llandudno LL30 2RP
Tel: 01492 871649

Here, delicious teas, coffees and cream
cakes are served by Victorian-style
waitresses known as Badgers' Nippies.
Welsh treats such as bara brith and
Welsh cakes are on the menu, along
with Welsh rarebit, swan meringues
and dragon eclairs.

The Buttery
8 High Street, Welshpool
SY21 7JP Tel: 01938 552658

Set in a black-and-white timbered
building dating back to the early 16th
century, this friendly café is open daily
for a wide variety of snacks and meals.
Families are welcome with children's
menus and smaller portions available.
Vegetarians can enjoy a range of
dishes including Stilton, broccoli
and mushroom lasagne.

Honey Pots Ceramic Café
18 Castle Street, Llangollen LL20 8NU
Tel: 01978 869008
www.honey-pots.com

At Honey Pots you can enjoy delicious
teas or coffees and tasty cakes and
snacks in smart modern surroundings
while admiring the views of Dinas
Bran's hilltop castle. When you have
had your fill of cakes you can turn your
hand to designing your own, unique
piece of pottery.

Britannia Inn

Horseshoe Pass, Llangollen LL20 8DW
Tel: 01978 860144
www.britinn.com

This cosy 14th-century inn, built by
the monks of nearby Valle Crucis, is
at the foot of the Horseshoe Pass with
fine views of the Vale of Llangollen. It
has open fires and beamed ceilings,
serves Theakston's ales and a good
selection of bar meals, including
favourites such as rump steak and
chicken Kiev. Children are very
welcome, as are well-behaved dogs.

Dragon Hotel

Montgomery SY15 6PA
Tel: 01686 668359
www.dragonhotel.com

The impressive black-and-white half-
timbered coaching inn in the heart
of the town offers an extensive menu
with blackboard specials. You'll find
good local produce including local
Welsh lamb and beef, a wide choice
for vegetarians, tasty pasta and game
dishes. The beers are from the local
Woods and Monty's breweries.

Grouse Inn

Carrog, Corwen LL21 9AT
Tel: 01490 430272

A splendidly sited inn looking across
the Dee and the Vale of Llangollen to
the Berwyn Mountains. A short walk
from Carrog station on the Llangollen
Steam Line, it has excellent cask ales
with a good menu and specials board.

Hawk & Buckle Inn

Llannefydd, Denbigh
LL16 5ED Tel: 01745 540249

The 17th-century coaching inn, situated
high up in the hills, is well known
for its fine cuisine and welcoming
ambience. There is an extensive menu,
which uses local lamb, beef, salmon
and vegetarian options.

West Arms

Llanarmon, Dyffryn Ceiriog LL20 7LD
Tel: 01691 600665

The West Arms is cosy and welcoming
with its beamed ceilings and roaring
log fires. Thanks to renowned chef
Grant Williams the cuisine is of
international standard.

Brecon Beacons & Mid Wales

ABERYSTWYTH &
  CEREDIGION COAST

ABERGAVENNY

BRECON & PEN Y FAN

GLYNTAWE & UPPER
  SWANSEA VALLEY

HAY-ON-WYE

LLANDOVERY &
  TYWI VALLEY

MACHYNLLETH

RHANDIRMWYN

RHAYADER

INTRODUCTION

Four great mountain ranges, the Black Mountain in the west, Fforest Fawr, the Brecon Beacons and the Black Mountains of the east, form the spine of the National Park and many of the sandstone escarpments have finely sculpted northern cliffs and instantly recognisable table-like summits. The Brecon Beacons valleys are fertile, with fields as green and lush as those of Ireland, but to the north the scenery transforms into the wild beauty of the remote hills and valleys of Mid Wales, a haven for those who are looking for tranquillity.

Unmissable attractions

Walk, climb or just stand and gaze across the Brecon Beacons' fertile valleys, with fields as green and lush as those of Ireland, or the wild remote hills and valleys of Mid Wales, a haven for those who like tranquillity and a more subtle beauty...explore Hay-on-Wye, a vibrant market town with a rich history, bookshops galore and an annual literary festival...get into the swing at the jazz festival in Brecon...cycle around the Elan Valley, an easy route along an old railway trackbed...visit the fascinating Centre for Alternative Technology in a disused Llwyngwern slate quarry.

2

1 Hay-on-Wye
The beautiful Wye Valley, including the stretch around Hay-on-Wye, is worthy of exploration.

2 Llandovery
A delightfully lush green countryside with rolling hills between Llandovery and the Brecon Beacons.

3 Elan Valley
The mighty Victorian dam of the Craig Goch reservoir holds back the waters of the Elan Valley.

4 Aberaeron
Pretty Aberaeron, south of Aberystwyth, is an ideal resort for coastal walkers to use as a base.

5 Brecon Beacons
Walking is the most popular activity in the Brecon Beacons with over 620 miles (1,000km) of public rights of way.

5

ABERYSTWYTH

ABERYSTWYTH & CEREDIGION COAST

Seen from the pier, Aberystwyth, the largest resort on Cardigan Bay, looks like any other typical British seaside town, with a pleasant arcing of the dark sand and pebble beach, neat rows of Victorian hotels and B&Bs, and a nice green hill rising behind at the far end. But Aberystwyth is more than this: it is a town of great historical importance and with more than a little culture.

In the 6th century, Celtic missionaries set up a small monastery at Llanbadarn, the original name for Aberystwyth, but the concentric rings of an ancient hill fort on the summit of Penparcau, clearly visible from the harbour, date back even further – to 600 BC.

Over the centuries the religious settlement would develop into a centre of learning, one that continues today with the University and the Library of Wales. Like most strategic places in Wales the town has its Norman castle, though this

147

one lies in ruins after it was blown up in 1649, just six years after it served as a Royal Mint for King Charles II. Many visitors take the short ride on the cliff railway to Constitution Hill, where there is café, a camera obscura, and a superb view of Aberystwyth and the whole of the Cardigan Bay coastline.

Visit

PLYNLIMON

Plynlimon (Pumlumon in Welsh) at 2468ft (752m) is at the heart of the Cambrian Mountains, a swathe of moors, ridges, vales and lakes encompassing Mid Wales. George Borrow, a 19th-century writer, loved the mountain, and sipped the water from the sources of its three great rivers, the Severn, the Wye and the Rheidol. Two corners of this wild mountain that are well worth visiting are the lake filled rocky corrie of Llyn Llygad Rheidol, and Glaslyn, a high windswept lake accessible by car from the Machynlleth–Llanidloes mountain road.

The Vale of Rheidol narrow-gauge railway, built in 1902, takes passengers on an hour-long journey to Devil's Bridge, revealing spectacular views of the wooded Rheidol Valley along the way. At Devil's Bridge coin-operated turnstiles either side of the road allow access to paths into a spectacular wooded gorge where you'll see three bridges, one on top of another (legend has it that the lowest one was built with the help of the Devil) and the Mynach Falls, which tumble from a great height past the treetops into the depths of the gorge far beneath your feet.

Further to the south along the coast from Aberystwyth are the pretty resorts of Aberaeron and Newquay. Aberaeron, a more sedate resort ideal for coast-walkers, has stylish colour-washed Georgian terraces overlooking the quay and riverside, while the busy but pretty little seaside town of Newquay is ideal for families with its excellent sandy beach and facilities.

ABERGAVENNY

Abergavenny, which is by far the largest town in the upper Usk Valley, occupies a large basin surrounded by three very distinctly shaped mountains: the cone-shaped Sugar Loaf Mountain and the craggy Ysgyryd Fawr in the north; Blorenge in the south. It's also well situated as a base to explore the Black Mountains and the Brecon Beacons. Although it took a pounding in the Civil War, Abergavenny's Norman castle is still worth seeing, as is the museum next door.

There's no shortage of castles in the surrounding area too. Raglan lies 10 miles (16km) east along the A40, while the lesser known 'three castles' of Grosmont, Skenfrith and White Castle are hidden away in low, rolling hills a few miles to the east. Along some of the narrowest country lanes imaginable in the beautiful Vale of Ewyas, lie the romantic ruins of Llanthony Priory founded by Augustinian canons early in the 12th century.

For visitors who find Abergavenny a little too busy – they do get traffic jams here – Crickhowell, further west up the Usk Valley, is a picturesque village that is almost as well sited for many of the tourist attractions in the area.

BRECON & PEN Y FAN

Although the Romans made their home here, Brecon's roots date back to the 5th century when it was governed by the Celtic chieftain, Brychan, who gave his name to the town. Situated at the confluences of the rivers Usk, Honddu and Tarell, the town grew in importance during Norman times when a Benedictine monastery, a castle and formidable town walls were built.

In the Act of Union of 1536 Brecon was listed as one of four local capitals and in 1542 Henry VIII set up a chancery here, installing the exchequer in the castle. Today, Brecon's castle stands as a battlemented wall set in the gardens of the Castle of Brecon Hotel.

The only fragments of the town wall still standing are near Captains Walk. St John's Church, part of the monastery, survived the Dissolution and in 1923 was elevated to cathedral status. The impressive old, red sandstone building was extensively refurbished in 1872 by Sir Gilbert Scott, whose finest work is the chancel's vaulted ceiling.

The town centre's buildings are a mixture of Georgian, Jacobean and Tudor, with a network of narrow streets leading off the Bulwark. The 19th-century Shire Hall with its Athenian-style columns, houses the lively and fascinating Brecknock Museum and Art Gallery, while Brecon's military history is well-recorded and celebrated at the Museums of the Royal Regiment of Wales in the Barracks.

Each August, Brecon swings to its own jazz festival, one of Britain's premier jazz events. For those who like old steam railways, the Brecon Mountain Railway puffs 7 miles (11km) from Pant just north of Merthyr Tydfil, into the foothills of the Brecon Beacons.

Seemingly always in view from the town and riverbanks, the Beacons' twin peaks, Pen y Fan (2,907ft/886m) and Corn Du (2,863ft/873m) display their angular outlines, finely sculpted northern cliffs and shadowy cwms to perfection. The proliferation of walking gear shops in the town shows that many visitors come to

Visit

WATERFALL COUNTRY

Four streams, the Nedd, Pyrddin, Mellte and Hepste, tumble down from the moors of Fforest Fawr to cut deep gorges through the more permeable limestone rocks. They create a series of spectacular waterfalls in the woods north of Pontneddfechan. All are approachable by footpath from car parks just south of the tiny village of Ystradfellte. At the most impressive fall, Sgwd yr Eira, visitors can walk behind the falls and look through the cascading water.

walk and there's no finer place than Brecon to explore southern Britain's highest mountains.

GLYNTAWE & UPPER SWANSEA VALLEY

The transition from stark industrial landscapes to rural ones happens very suddenly in the Swansea Valley. One minute you're in Ystradgynlais on the edge of the old coalfields, the next you've turned the corner past Abercraf into the magical garden-like landscapes of Glyntawe and you're staring across the River Tawe up to the limestone crags of Cribarth, a southern outlier of the Black Mountain. Glyntawe, a sprawling village, is one of the best starting points for a climb on the Fan Hir escarpment to the highest Black Mountain summit, Fan Brycheiniog.

The limestone geology of the valley has left it with its major attraction, the Dan yr Ogof Caves, discovered in 1912. This is Wales' largest subterranean cavern system, where visitors can enter a weird world of impressive stalactites, stalagmites and underground waterfalls brought to life with lighting and music. The south side of the valley is dominated by Craig y Nos Castle, once home to world-famous Victorian opera singer Adelina Patti. This Gothic mansion, now a grand hotel, is surrounded by superb riverside gardens with mature woodland fringing meres and meadows that now form a valuable part of the Craig y Nos Country Park.

HAY-ON-WYE

Hay-on-Wye lies in the northeast corner of the Brecon Beacons National Park, by the sleepy banks of the River Wye and sheltered by the sweeping slopes of the Black Mountains. With the flower-decked meadows and rolling green hills of Radnorshire in the north, spring and summer in Hay are delightful times.

The name hay comes from the Norman word *haie* meaning 'enclosed place'. It is known that there was a settlement here when

Visit

THE DINAS NATURE RESERVE

This RSPB reserve, which lies 10 miles (16km) north of Llandovery and south of Llyn Brianne, has a footpath over wetlands and through oak woodland to the steep slopes of Dinas. There's a cave in the crags here, where Twm Sion Catti, the Welsh Robin Hood, used to hide from his enemies. Red kites can often be seen soaring above the trees and in summer, you can also see dippers, pied flycatchers, common sandpipers and grey wagtails.

The area around Llandovery was once occupied by the Romans, whose fort, Alabum, was sited near to St Mary's Church by the Afon Bran to the north of the town. The castle, which was built for the Norman baron Richard Fitz Pons in the 12th century, was captured by the Welsh in the Glyndwr Revolts. In 1532 its owner, Rhys-ap-Gruffydd, was executed at the hands of Henry VIII for treason and, in an act of revenge by the Welsh, the castle was destroyed, never to be rebuilt. A recently erected statue of Llywelyn ap Gruffydd stands guard on the grassy bank beneath the remains of the castle keep. Across the car park from the statue you'll find the Heritage Centre where you can get information about the many walks in the area and discover the myths and history of the region.

Llandovery's history is intertwined with the fortunes of the cattle drovers. When thieves made travelling on Wales' rugged roads a hazardous exercise, the local farmers hired the drovers to drive cattle to the more lucrative markets of England and to settle accounts for them with non-local people. This meant that drovers needed to handle large sums of money and led to the introduction of banking systems some of them even issuing bank notes. One of the most successful of these was David Jones' Black Ox Bank, which was taken over at the turn of the 20th century by Lloyds.

Visit

CENTRE FOR ALTERNATIVE TECHNOLOGY

The Centre for Alternative Technology was founded in 1973 and utilised the disused Llwyngwern slate quarry, a couple of miles (3.2km) north of Machynlleth. From very small beginnings, the centre now has a workforce of 90 permanent staff and volunteers on the 7-acre (2.8ha) site. Visitors to the centre can get up the hill on an amazing water-powered cliff railway. They will see exciting interactive displays about global issues such as energy generation and transport, along with some practical ideas for their own homes and lifestyles, including organic gardening.

To the south of Llandovery, the Black Mountain (or Mynydd Du as it is known in Wales) lies at the western end of the Brecon Beacon Range, rising in grand escarpments of old red sandstone. Glacial action has formed magnificent cliffs on the northern and eastern faces of the group and also provided two lovely tarns: Llyn y Fan Fawr and Llyn y Fan Fach. Myddfai, which is sheltered in the northern foothills of the Black Mountain, is a particularly picturesque village with a fine 13th-century church. The nearby Epynt army ranges are encircled by a recreational bridlepath and footpath.

MACHYNLLETH

Machynlleth shelters on high ground to the south of the wide valley of the Dyfi, where the mountains of Snowdonia give way to the rolling foothills of Plynlimon. A fine 17th-century four-arched stone bridge spans the river on the road leading into this small market town. An ornately designed 80-foot (24m) Victorian clock tower forms the hub of this town and looks down on a wide Maengwyn Street, where the weekly Wednesday markets are held. Here you'll also find Parliament House, a medieval town house standing on the site of the building where Owain Glyndwr held the last independent Welsh Parliament in 1404. It now hosts an Owain Glyndwr interpretative centre. The early 14th-century Royal House, at the junction of Garsiwn Lane and Penrallt Street, is where Charles I stayed in 1644.

Today Machynlleth has an appealing mix of all things Welsh, Celtic mysticism and green idealism. The unusual shops and the wholefood café are a testament to this, as is the Centre for Alternative Technology. The townsfolk were a bit dubious when the 'hippies' first set up the alternative living centre, but their fortunes are now intertwined.

North of the town, the Dulas Valley threads past the Centre for Alternative Technology into a countryside of swift streams, forests and fractured mountains where slate was mined for centuries. At Corris, a narrow-gauge railway (closed 1948) is being resurrected; into the hills, hamlets crouch beneath spectacular landscapes, a paradise for the path-finding rambler.

Insight

THE PHYSICIANS OF MYDDFAI

Llyn y Fan Fach at the northern foot of the Black Mountain is an eerie place to be when the mists swirl around the gullies, and it's not surprising that there's some mystery and legend lurking beneath its waters. From its depths a flaxen-haired fairy appeared and enchanted a local farmer's boy, Rhiwallon. After altercations with her husband the fairy returned to the waters. However, the couple sired three sons, who would learn from their mother about medicine. The boys became the first in a line of Physicians of Myddfai, the last was Dr C Rice Williams of Aberystwyth, who died in 1842.

RHANDIRMWYN

Once an important old lead-mining village, Rhandirmwyn lies in the valley of the Upper Tywi, 9 miles (14km) north of Llandovery and the A40. This is a real haven for those who like riverside walks, angling and bird-spotting. Two fine bird reserves

161

LLYN BRIANNE

are set scenically among the riverside crags, where the boisterous Tywi and Doethie rivers twist and turn between rocky, oak-clad peaks. Beneath the conical hill called Dinas, the rivers converge in a violent cauldron of foam.

A short distance upstream, where the Doethie meets the Pysgotwr, is one of the wildest gorges in Mid Wales. Just a few miles north of Rhandirmwyn along winding country lanes, Llyn Brianne Reservoir is surrounded by plantations of spruce and larch in two narrow valleys, those of the Tywi and Camddwr.

RHAYADER

Rhayader's full Welsh name is Rhaeadr Gwy, meaning 'waterfall on the Wye'. The waterfall to which it refers was actually blown up in 1780 to make way for the bridge over the river. Dominated by its opulent Victorian clock tower, which lies at the crossroads in the centre of the village, Rhayader is a very pleasant

Visit

GIGRIN FARM RED KITE FEEDING STATION

Gigrin Farm, an upland sheep farm on the A470, 0.6 mile (1km) south of Rhayader, is an official RSPB feeding station for red kites. It's fascinating to see first the noisy crows arriving on the scene, then the red kites and buzzards swooping down at break-neck speed to foil the smaller birds. The number of kites visiting the feeding station can vary from a dozen to around 400 or so. Feeding the birds takes place every afternoon.

and Caban-coch were constructed. Nantgwyllt was among the dwellings submerged by the reservoirs. Its garden walls can still be seen when Caban-coch's water levels are low. A church, chapel, school and numerous farms were submerged when the scheme was completed in 1904. A fifth reservoir, the Claerwen, was completed in 1952. One hundred years later, the reservoirs have blended almost seamlessly with their surroundings and the power of the dams, and the white waters thundering down them, add great character to the landscape.

The visitor centre gives an intriguing insight into the construction of the dams, the railway built to supply them and the lives of the construction workers involved in the project. The old railway trackbed now forms the Elan Valley Trail, which is a marvellous facility for waterside walking, cycling and horse riders. The trail has been intended to open access to the Elan Valley especially for the less able.

town set among some of the finest river scenery in Mid Wales. The poet Percy Shelley was drawn to these parts in 1809. He lived in the cottage of Nantgwyllt in the Elan Valley, then a famed beauty spot. However, the planned flooding of the Elan Valley was to change the nature of the scenery forever. In the first part of the scheme, four reservoirs, the Craig Goch, Penygarreg, Carreg-ddu

ELAN VALLEY

BRECON BEACONS & MID WALES

TOURIST INFORMATION CENTRES

Abergavenny
Swan Meadow.
Tel: 01873 853254

Aberystwyth
Terrace Road.
Tel: 01970 612125

Brecon
Cattle Market Car Park.
Tel: 01874 622485

Hay-on-Wye
Oxford Road.
Tel: 01497 820144

Llandovery
Heritage Centre, Kings Road.
Tel: 01550 720693

Llandrindod Wells
Old Town Hall, Memorial Gardens.
Tel: 01597 822600

Machynlleth
Canolfan Owain Glyndwr.
Tel: 01654 702401

Rhayader
The Leisure Centre, North Street.
Tel: 01597 810591

PLACES OF INTEREST

Brecon Cathedral
Cathedral Close, Brecon, Powys.
Tel: 01874 623857;
www.breconcathedral.org.uk

Carreg Cennen Castle
Trapp, Nr Llandeilo.
Tel: 01558 822291. Perhaps Wales'
most spectacularly sited castle.

Centre for Alternative Technology
Machynlleth. Tel: 01654 705950;
www.cat.org.uk
See some of the solutions to the
challenges facing Earth.

Ceredigion Museum/Coliseum Gallery
Coliseum, Terrace Road, Aberystwyth,
Dyfed. Tel: 01970 633088
Objects from the historic industries of
the people of Ceredigion.

Dan-yr-Ogof Showcaves
Brecon Road, Penycae.
Tel: 01639 730284;
www.showcaves.co.uk
Underground stalagmites, stalactites,
waterfalls, museum and dinosaur park.

Dinas Nature Reserve
Rhandirmwyn. RSPB reserve with
walk, shop, visitor centre. Car charges.

Dolaucothi Gold Mines
Pumpsaint, Llanwrda,
Carmarthenshire. (Site off A482
between Lampeter and Llanwrda.)
Tel: 01558 650177. Free for NT
members (excludes underground tour).
Only known Roman gold mine in UK.

Gigrin Farm Kite Feeding Station
South St, Rhayader. Tel: 01597 810243;
www.gigrin.co.uk
See the red kite close up.

National Cycle Collection
The Automobile Palace,
Temple Street, Llandrindod Wells.
Tel: 01597 825531;
www.cyclemuseum.org.uk
From penny farthings to modern bikes.

National Library of Wales
Penglais, Aberystwyth.
Tel: 01970 623816. Includes exhibitions
(some free), cinema and a restaurant.

FOR CHILDREN
Borth Animalarium
North of Aberystwyth.
Tel: 01970 871224;
www.animalarium.co.uk
A rescue zoo for exotic animals.

Brecon Mountain Railway
Pant Station, Merthyr Tydfil.
Tel: 01685 722988;
www.breconmountainrailway.co.uk
A narrow-gauge steam line.

Vale of Rheidol Railway
Park Avenue, Aberystwyth.
Tel: 01970 625819;
www.rheidolrailway.co.uk
One of the Great Little Trains of Wales.

SHOPPING
Market Days
Abergavenny, Tue; Farmers'
market, 2nd and 4th Thu of month.
Aberystwyth, 1st and 3rd Sat of month;
Brecon, Tue and Fri.
Hay-on-Wye, Thu.
Lampeter, alternate Fri.
Llandovery, Farmers' market last Sat.
Llandrindod Wells, Fri; Farmers'
market last Thu of the month.
Llanidloes, Sat.
Machynlleth, Wed.

PERFORMING ARTS

Aberystwyth Arts Centre
The University of Wales, Aberystwyth,
Penglais Campus, Aberystwyth.
Tel: 01970 623232;
www.aberystwythartscentre.co.uk

The Tabernacle
Penrallt St, Machynlleth, Powys.
Tel: 01654 703355;
www.momawales.co.uk

Theatr Brycheiniog
Canal Wharf, Brecon.
Tel: 01874 611622

Theatr Hafren
Llanidloes Rd, Newtown, SY16 4HX.
Tel: 01686 625007;
www.theatrhafren.com

SPORTS & ACTIVITIES

ANGLING

Freshwater
Opportunities for fishing on farms,
lakes and rivers, including the Clwydog
Reservoir near Llanidloes, the Beacons
Reservoir and the River Tawe in
Carmarthenshire. Permits and
licences are available from tackle
shops and TICs.

BOAT TRIPS

Beaon Park Day Boats
Brecon. Tel: 0800 612 2890;
www.beaconparkdayboats.co.uk
Self-drive on Monmouthshire
& Brecon Canal.

New Quay Boat Trips
New Quay. Tel: 01545 560800;
www.newquayboattrips.co.uk
Watch dolphins, seals and sealife
in Cardigan Bay.

CANOEING
Glasbury-on-Wye.
Tel: 01497 847213;
www.wyevalleycanoes.co.uk

CYCLING

Cycle Routes
Taff Trail (Cardiff to Brecon Beacons).
Elan Valley Trail (Rhayader
to Elan Reservoirs).
Ystwyth Trail (Aberystwyth
to Tregaron, 21 miles).
Nant yr Arian Forest (Aberystwyth).

Cycle Hire
Three Cocks. Tel: 01497 847897;
www.blackmountain.co.uk
Brecon. Tel: 01874 610071;
www.bikesandhikes.co.uk

GOLF

Borth & Ynyslas Golf Club
Aer y Mor, Borth.
Tel: 01970 871202. 18 holes.

Cradoc Golf Club
Penoyre Park, Cradoc, Brecon.
Tel: 01874 623658
18 holes.

Machynlleth Golf Club
Newtown Rd, Machynlleth.
Tel: 01654 702000. 9 holes.

Rhosgoch Golf Club
Rhosgoch, Builth Wells.
Tel: 01497 851251. 18 holes.

St Idloes Golf Club
Trefeglwys Rd, Llanidloes.
Tel: 01686 412559. 9 holes.

HORSE RIDING

Cantref Riding Centre
Cantref, Brecon.
Tel: 01874 665223;
www.cantref.com

Mills Bros
New Court, Felindre,
Three Cocks, Brecon.
Tel: 01497 847285

Underhill Riding Stables
Underhill Farm, Dolau,
Llandrindod Wells.
Tel: 01597 851890

WALKING

Long Distance Routes
The Beacons Way. Glyndwr's Way.
Offa's Dyke Path. Wye Valley Walk.

FESTIVALS & EVENTS

Brecon Jazz festival
Tel: 0870 990 1299;
www.breconjazz.org
mid-Aug.

Hay Festival
Tel: 01497 822629;
www.hayfestival.co.uk
Literary festival, end May
to early Jun.

Musicfest Aberystwyth
Displays, music and dancing
www.aberfest.org, end Jul.

Royal Welsh Show
Builth Wells. Tel: 01982 553683;
www.rwas.co.uk
Agricultural show, mid to
end Jul.

TEA ROOMS

Giglios Coffee Shop
10 Bethel Square, Brecon LD3 7JP
Tel: 01874 625062
A modern licensed coffee shop and restaurant in the heart of Brecon. Excellent cream teas, gateaux and sandwiches, such as smoked salmon and cream cheese, Thai green chicken, or salmon with dill mayonnaise.

The Granary
20 Broad Street,
Hay-on-Wye HR3 5DB
Tel: 01497 820790
The splendid licensed café has a cosy bistro-style interior with outside tables looking across to the town's Victorian clocktower. Food includes sandwiches, jacket potatoes and warming soups as well as full main meals.

Hive on the Quay
Aberaeron, Ceredigion
SA46 0BT
Tel: 01545 570445
www.hiveonthequay.co.uk
On the picturesque harbour and close to the Ceredigion Coastal Footpath; a chance to work up an appetite for a ploughman's with local cheeses, a savoury stuffed pancake, home-made honey ice cream or a local fish chowder. Boats based at the port land Cardigan Bay crab.

The Quarry Shop and Café
Maengwyn Street
Machynlleth SY20 8EB
Tel: 01654 702624
A very popular wholefood vegetarian café set up by the Centre for Alternative Technology. They only use seasonal, organic and Fairtrade produce. Their date slices are absolutely delicious and the soups will warm you.

THE HAY BOOK COMPANY

explore
four
floors......

ADMIRABLE
GENERAL
BOOKS

explore

four
floors......

Harbourmaster Hotel
Aberaeron SA46 0BA
Tel: 01545 570755
www.harbour-master.com

The hotel restaurant prides itself on its use of local produce, including Aberaeron prawns and mackerel, Cardigan Bay crab and lobster, Welsh Black beef and venison. All this plus Welsh microbrewery beers and a good bin of wines.

Harp Inn
Old Radnor LD8 2RH
Tel: 01544 350655
www.harpinnradnor.co.uk

In beautiful countryside close to Hergest Ridge, this renovated 15th-century Welsh longhouse is a classic village inn, all flagstones, fires, beams and settles. Popular with pony-trekkers for beers from Bishop's Castle or Ludlow breweries; a great menu of classics and modern dishes seals the deal here.

Kilvert's Hotel
The Bull Ring, Hay-on-Wye HR3 5AG
Tel: 01497 821042
www.kilverts.co.uk

The ivy-clad Georgian free house is popular with locals and tourists alike, with a small flagged outdoor terrace area in the front, a rustic oak-beamed bar serving real ales such as Breconshire Brewery's Kilvert's Gold, along with bar meals like slow-roasted Welsh lamb, pizzas and pastas. The elegant restaurant specialises in lamb and fish.

Royal Oak
Rhandirmwyn, Llandovery SA20 0NY
Tel: 01550 760201

A proper old-fashioned country pub overlooking the Tywi Valley and mountains. Stone and tile floors and an open fire give the bar a rustic atmosphere, while the restaurant is decorated in cottage style. In summer there's a pleasant garden. Meals include venison casserole, Welsh Black beef and chicken curry.

Pembrokeshire

INTRODUCTION

In Welsh Pen-Fro means
land's end and, fittingly,
Pembrokeshire's sinuous
coastline reaches out into
the waves of the Atlantic
Ocean like a gnarled fist.
Volcanic eruptions and earth
movements have left a tortured
rocky coastline of some 160
miles (260km), whose beauty
and drama have been
recognised by National Park
status. In Pembrokeshire
you can take it easy on the
sandy beaches, make sport
out of those Atlantic waves,
or discover the mysteries
of St David's or the ancient
Preseli Hills.

NEWGALE BEACH

ESSENTIAL SIGHTS

Unmissable attractions

Explore Milford Haven, described by Admiral Lord Nelson as one of the world's finest harbours...walk across the Preseli Hills and look out for the famous blue dolomite stones that were transported from here to Wiltshire to build Stonehenge or seek out Pentre Ifan, Britain's largest and best-preserved burial chamber...explore St David's, Britain's smallest city...enjoy fantastic walking and birdwatching around the Marloes Peninsula...or take a ferry trip to Skomer Island from Martin's Haven and relish the views of puffins, dolphins and, possibly, basking sharks...experience Fishguard's Music Festival in June or Tenby's Arts Festival in September...discover Solva, one of Pembrokeshire's most picturesque and popular resorts.

2

3

1 Pembroke
Magnificent Pembroke Castle occupies a commanding position between two tidal inlets.

2 Tenby
Boats trips from Tenby harbour offer the chance to see grey seals.

3 Marloes Sands
This spectacular beach, in sight of Skomer and Skokholm Islands, is cared for by the National Trust.

179

HAVERFORDWEST & ST BRIDES BAY

Sited on the Western Cleddau, one of the two wide rivers that flow into the Milford Haven, Haverfordwest was, before the arrival of the railways, a thriving port with barges, small steamships and coasting vessels regularly docking on the quayside. The castle, built by the first Earl of Pembroke, Gilbert de Clare in the 12th century, dominates the town from a lofty crag above the river.

As a Norman stronghold, Haverfordwest was attacked and burned to the ground by Llywelyn the Great, but the castle survived, as it did when besieged in 1405 by another Prince of Wales, Owain Glyndwr. However, Oliver Cromwell ordered its destruction following the Civil War. Nevertheless, the substantial walls and keep remain an impressive sight – second only to Pembroke in this region.

Today Haverfordwest is a thriving market town, the principal shopping centre for the area. Many shops and a café line the quayside. It's worth visiting the town museum, which is housed in the castle off Church Street. Also worth seeing are the recently excavated ruins of the Augustinian Priory of St Mary and St Thomas the Martyr, a short walk from the town centre.

Haverfordwest is an excellent base from which to explore Pembrokeshire's West Coast and St Brides Bay. Facing west to the Atlantic, most of the St Brides beaches are exposed to the prevailing winds. This whips up the surf and makes them extremely popular for sports such as surfing, windsurfing and kite-surfing. The most northerly of these is Newgale Sands, where a splendid golden beach stretches 2 miles (3km) from Newgale village in the north to the rocks of Rickets Head. A tall shingle bank separates the beach from the village. Patrolling lifeguards designate the safe swimming areas.

There's another long sandy beach at Broadhaven, a lively resort

Visit

SKOMER

There's a summer ferry (not Mondays) to Skomer Island from Martin's Haven on the headland west of Marloes. On the short voyage you may be lucky enough to see porpoises and dolphins, or even a basking shark. You'll almost certainly see some of the 6,000 breeding pairs of puffins peeping from their burrows. Like much of the mainland Skomer Island is girt with dark volcanic cliffs, which accommodate southern Britain's largest colony of nesting seabirds. On the pink thrift and sea campion-decked clifftops are the remnants of an Iron Age civilisation – a standing stone, burial cairns, ancient field boundaries and the earthworks of hut circles. A number of footpaths criss-cross the island. Do not stray off the paths.

with a good range of facilities. It's worth exploring the northern end to see natural rock arches and stacks. To the south lies Little Haven. This pretty village with a slipway, used by the lifeboat, and beach, is a popular place with sea anglers.

Most spectacular is Marloes Sands where violent earth movements thrust up the rock strata to form steeply angled rocky cliffs that resemble yacht sails caught in a great gust of wind. Marloes village is a 0.6-mile (1km) walk from the isolated sandy beach.

MILFORD HAVEN

'It's one of the world's finest harbours,' Admiral Lord Nelson claimed as he gazed admiringly across the vast blue waters of Milford Haven. And this lovely sheltered estuary has provided one of Britain's most important maritime strongholds since the days of the Tudor kings. And yet Milford Haven the town is a more recent affair, built and planned in the late 18th century by Sir William Hamilton, the husband of Nelson's mistress, Emma. In the 1960s the big ships arrived – carrying crude oil for processing in new refineries.

Of these, only the Texaco plant now survives. Today Milford boasts a pleasant harbour front and marina, overlooked by the Georgian buildings of Hamilton Terrace. In 1991 memories were rekindled when the Tall Ships Race came to town.

NEWPORT

While its next-door neighbour Fishguard is bustling with cars and lorries rushing to make the ferry to Ireland on time, life in little Newport, tucked away in the far northwest corner of Pembrokeshire, chugs along at a more relaxed pace. Here the distinctive crag-topped Carn Ingli ('Angel Mountain') rises from the back gardens of the villagers' cottages, while small boats bobble from their moorings or lean against the sandbars of the Nevern Estuary. Although only 1,138-feet (347m) high Carn Ingli is distinctively rugged and its cloak of heather and gorse is capped by jagged outcrops of dolerite. The ramparts that remain from an Iron Age fort ring the

Visit

BURIAL CROMLECH

Pentre Ifan is probably the finest example of a neolithic burial cromlech in Wales. It dates back to around 3500 BC and its huge capstone measures over 16 feet (5m) long poised on three 8-foot (2.5m) uprights, which seem to frame Carn Ingli's mystical outlines to perfection. The cromlech can be seen free of charge and is well signposted from the A487 east of Newport and the B4329 Preseli road at Brynberian. Near by is Castell Henllys Iron Age Fort.

summit of the hill, which is scattered with the foundations of those early settlers' circular huts.

Newport Castle is part fortress, part manor house – it has been inhabited as a private dwelling for the past 150 years. Built in the 13th century by Norman baron William Fitzmartin, the castle was held for centuries by the powerful lords of Cemaes. As can be seen from its ruined battlements, the fortress

was often involved in bloody conflict, first in 1215 when captured and sacked by Llywelyn the Great, Prince of Wales, then by Owain Glyndwr. Fitzmartin also established St Mary's Church, whose impressive Norman square tower vies for dominance with the castle.

The River Nevern divides Newport's two beaches. On the north side there's an excellent sandy beach with safe bathing away from the currents of the river mouth. Parrog beach on the south side is for walkers who can stroll along the clifftops, past thickets of colourful gorse and shimmering sea pinks.

PEMBROKE

Pembroke is an attractive walled town with a 900-year history dating back to its Norman castle, which overlooks the town from its perch on a limestone crag. Surrounded by water on three sides, the castle, built by the Earls of Pembroke, was one of the biggest and most powerful in Wales. The walls of the

Visit

THE GUN TOWER MUSEUM

Built in 1851 to protect the Royal Naval Dockyard at Pembroke, the Gun Tower, which juts out into the wide waterway, now houses a museum illustrating Pembroke's military heritage. You can learn about life as experienced by one of Queen Victoria's soldiers who waited for an invasion that never came, see superb models of the old navy dockyard where more than 200 ships were built, and learn about the Second World War flying boats – Pembroke was the world's largest flying boat base.

keep are 7 feet (2m) thick and 75 feet (23m) high. A secret underground passage burrows beneath the Great Hall to the harbour. Harry Tudor, the grandson of John of Gaunt and a descendant of Llywelyn the Great, was born in Pembroke Castle. On returning from exile he advanced with an army that defeated Richard III at Bosworth Field, after which he was crowned King Henry VII.

In 1977 Pembroke was given Outstanding Conservation Area status. In the bustling main street, lined with both Georgian and Tudor buildings, there are some fascinating shops, cafés and restaurants. If it's peace you're after, a stroll by the river and Mill Pond will take you around the castle walls.

PRESELI HILLS

The Preseli Hills rise from Cardigan Bay at Fishguard and Newport and reach their highest point at Foel Cwmcerwyn some 1,760 feet (536m) above sea level. They're not that high by Welsh standards but these peaks have always been synonymous with all things spiritual. Preseli has sunsets that light up the whole of Cardigan Bay with a fiery glow, framed by the jagged silhouettes of strangely weathered summit tors.

Buried beneath your feet are the settlers from pre-history: the neolithic tribes who were here before the 'true Welsh', the Celts, came from across the sea.

Cromlechs, the earthwork and stone remains of fortress walls and hut circles are liberally scattered across the map for you to discover. The World Heritage Site of Stonehenge in Wiltshire was built from the rocks hewn from the Preselis. The rock that the monoliths were carved from, an igneous spotted dolerite, is exclusive to Carnmenyn on the eastern side of the range.

When the Normans attacked Pembrokeshire they built a line of castles from Pembroke to Roch near St Davids. The Welsh were driven into the foothills of the Preseli and an imaginary line, the Landsker, was to divide the different tongues. If you've first visited the county's English-speaking south coast you may be surprised when you arrive at Rosebush, a tiny village that lies to the south of Foel Cwmcerwyn, for this friendly place is Welsh-speaking. The little village, which is the starting point for the best Preseli walks, has a campsite and one of the best inns in Wales, Tafarn y Sinc.

Activity

RAMSEY ISLAND

You can take the regular Ramsey Island boat from the slipway at St Justinian's, just 3 miles (5km) west of St David's and you will be transported across the fast-flowing Sound and infamous reef known as the Bitches to a haven for wildlife. Ramsey Island's rugged coastline, with its 300-foot (91m) cliffs and isolated rock coves, is home to the largest colony of grey seals in southwest Britain. Two small hills provide exhilarating walks with panoramas of Pembrokeshire's coast and islands through to the distant Preseli Hills.

ST DAVID'S

Set on a windswept plateau, St David's, Britain's smallest city, is as isolated from urban life as it is possible to be. Flanked on either side by jagged dolerite crests of Carn Llidi and Carnedd-lleithr, this looks and feels as if it is an inhospitable corner of the world. And so it was when Dewi, a 6th-century Celtic preacher who was later to become St David, patron saint of Wales, sailed from Ireland to set up his monastery here.

When you arrive in St David's and walk up the High Street past the gift shops, cottages, the boat-trip vendors' offices and the cafés, there are no signs of the grand ecclesiastical buildings. They're hidden in the hollow of the Alun Valley, behind Cross Square, and it's only when you descend down the Pebbles to the Bell Tower that they appear. At first glance the cathedral is as austere as the surrounding landscape, yet the purple-hued sandstone and perfect proportions give it an impressive presence. Inside, the cathedral is light and airy, with fine ornamental Norman arches and slightly leaning piers of the nave leading the eye to a splendid roof of Irish oak.

Destroyed several times by the violent Viking raids in pre-Norman days, the oldest part of the current cathedral, the nave, dates back to

1180 – the original tower collapsed in 1220. In the early 14th century Bishop Henry de Gower raised the walls of the aisles, inserted much grander windows and built the south porch, transept chapels and Lady Chapel. A century later Bishop Vaughan built up the tower to its present height and added the splendid roof.

The Reformation left the cathedral neglected and it was damaged during the Civil War. In 1862 George Gilbert Scott was charged with renovating the cathedral. While doing so he discovered two skeletons, believed to be St David and his friend St Justinian, now kept in an oak chest in the Holy Trinity Chapel.

For around nine days in May and June each year, St David's Cathedral holds a festival of classical music. St David's three cathedral choirs attend, as well as many top musicians from around the world.

Across the Alun stream lie the large and magnificent ruins of the Bishop's Palace. The palace was built in the late 12th century, but significantly enlarged by Bishop Henry de Gower between 1328 and 1347 to accommodate the growing number of pilgrims who flocked to St David's each year. St David's became a seat of power, illustrated by the opulent arcaded parapets and the magnificence of the Great Hall. Today the palace is often a venue for concerts and plays. There are two permanent exhibitions: the Lords of the Palace and Life in the Palace of a Prince of the Church.

SAUNDERSFOOT

Once a small fishing village, which flourished with finds of high quality anthracite coal, Saundersfoot has since been caught up in near neighbour Tenby's popularity. It's not hard to see why. Set at the foot of a pleasant wooded valley, the village has an attractive harbour alongside wonderful golden sands. The village is a popular centre for fishing, sailing and water sports.

SOLVA

Three miles (5km) east of St David's lies Solva, a village of two parts. The more modern upper village lines the A487 coast road, while in the lower, more attractive part, cottages, small shops and restaurants cluster around the harbour at the sheltered head of a long, winding tidal inlet. These days Solva is a busy little tourist trap but it was founded on maritime traditions. A thriving port until the arrival of the railways, it had several warehouses and a dozen or so limekilns. Solva once boasted a passenger service to New York. However, rather unusually, the passengers would have to bring their own food for a voyage that could last for up to four months!

Though it's a fine place for pottering about and having a spot of lunch, Solva is one of the best bases for a coastal walk, maybe to St David's (get the bus back), or just a stroll along the Gribin, where there's an Iron Age settlement and a perfect view back to the village.

STACKPOLE

The 2,000-acre (810ha) estate, once owned by the powerful Scottish Cawdor family but now managed by the National Trust, is situated between Bosherton, Stackpole and St Govan's Head. It encompasses some of Pembrokeshire's finest coastal scenery.

Bosherton, a tiny village at the western end of the estate, is well situated for a visit to the Bosherton Lily Ponds. These were created by flooding three wooded limestone valleys. It has been claimed that this was the home of the Lady of the Lake and from where King Arthur gained his magical sword, Excalibur. It's certainly a magical place for nature lovers, who can wander through the surrounding woodland at the water's edge to reach the seashore at Broad Haven beach. A June visit will reveal water lilies in full splendour, covering the waters of the Western Arm. Visitors include the cormorant, grey heron, kingfisher, coot and moorhen and

you're likely to see one of the many dragonfly, darting across the lakes.

There's another National Trust car park (toll) at Stackpole Quay near to the site of Stackpole Court. The mansion was demolished in 1963 when punitive taxes made it necessary for the Cawdors to dispose of their Welsh assets. The quay, a tiny inlet with a stone-built harbour pier, marks a clearly visible transition between the old red sandstone cliffs of Manorbier and the limestone of southwest Pembrokeshire. A short walk across fields and clifftops leads to some steps descending into Barafundle Bay, a traffic-free golden sandy beach ideal for swimming or a spot of sunbathing. Further expeditions through the pines and sycamores at the far end of the bay will take you to the cliffs, arches and stacks of Stackpole Head.

If you time your visit for when the military are not training, you can take the minor road leading south from Bosherton to St Govan's

Visit

STACK ROCKS AND THE GREEN BRIDGE OF WALES

Probably the most photographed feature on the Pembrokeshire coastline is the Green Bridge of Wales, a huge natural arch formed by the collapsing of two coastal caverns. It can be viewed from the safe platform on Stack Rocks, which are also known as Elegug Stacks. Before setting out along the road west of Castlemartin barracks, find out if the military are on exercise (Tel: 01646 662367).

car park. Steps lead down to the 13th-century St Govan's Chapel, a tiny building wedged into a fissure at the base of the cliffs on the site of a Celtic hermit's cell. St Govan, an 11th-century saint, is believed to have been buried beneath the altar.

TENBY

By far the biggest and most popular of Pembrokeshire's resorts, Tenby is surrounded by caravan sites.

197

Activity

CALDEY ISLAND

A boat trip from Tenby to Caldey Island is like a journey back in time, with quiet tracks wending through fields of barley and footpaths seeking out secluded cliff-ringed coves. In 1929 Cistercian monks re-established a monastery on Caldey. They farm the island's 600 acres (240ha) and make perfume from the flowers and herbs. Walkers can seek out the ruins of the old priory or climb to lofty vantage points for stunning views of the coast.

The place often buzzes with coach parties and holiday-makers from all backgrounds. On Bank Holidays the town feels like it's going to burst with the weight of its own popularity. But Tenby has undeniable beauty. Brightly colour-washed cottages wrap themselves around a small sandy beach, framed by the pier of the lifeboat station, the harbour and the small boats in the bay. When the coaches have gone you can take an after-dinner stroll on the promenade with those cottages and the old castle floodlit against the night sky.

Tenby has two distinct parts. Within the largely intact medieval town walls many ancient narrow streets have been cobbled to re-create their authenticity, but outside of these walls, overlooking the large South Beach, the Victorians' influence is there for all to see, with traditional seaside terraces. Castle Hill looks down on both the old and new towns, but little remained of the castle after its destruction in the Civil War. Much of the town's history can be traced at the Tenby Museum and Art Gallery on Castle Hill. This includes charters and privileges granted by the Tudors and the Earls of Pembroke.

A devised town trail visits the walls and many of the historic buildings, including the Tudor Merchant's House (National Trust), which is fitted out with authentic furnishings and has three walls with the remains of early frescoes.

PEMBROKESHIRE

TOURIST INFORMATION CENTRES

For general information go to
www.visitpembrokeshire.com

Fishguard
Town Hall.
Tel: 01437 776636

Haverfordwest
19 Old Bridge Street.
Tel: 01437 763110

Newport (seasonal)
2 Bank Cottages, Long Street.
Tel: 01239 820912

Pembroke
Commons Road.
Tel: 01646 622388

St David's
Oriel y Parc.
Tel: 01437 720392

Saundersfoot (seasonal)
Harbour Car Park.
Tel: 01834 813672

Tenby
Upper Park Road.
Tel: 01834 842404

PLACES OF INTEREST

Caldey Island
Off Tenby. Tel: 01834 844453;
www.caldey-island.co.uk
Take a boat trip from Tenby. Cistercian
monastery, quiet walks, and fine
beaches.

Castell Henllys
Off the A487 between Newport
(Pembrokeshire) and Cardigan.
Tel: 01239 891319;
www.castellhenllys.com

The Gun Tower Museum
Pembroke Dock.
Tel: 01646 622246
Pembrokeshire's naval heritage.

Pembroke Castle
Tel: 01646 684585;
www.pembrokecastle.co.uk

St David's Bishop's Palace
St David's, Pembrokeshire.
Tel: 01437 720517
Extensive and impressive ruins next
to cathedral. The entry fee includes
'Lords of the Palace' exhibition.

St David's Cathedral
St David's.
www.stdavidscathedral.org.uk

**Tenby Museum
and Art Gallery**
Castle Hill, Tenby.
Tel: 01834 842809;
www.tenbymuseum.org.uk

FOR CHILDREN
Dinosaur Park
Gumfreston, Tenby.
Tel: 01834 45272;
www.thedinosaurpark.co.uk
A 1-mile (1.6km) long walk complete
with prehistoric monsters and
woodland trail.
Folly Farm
Begelly, Kilgetty.
Tel: 01834 812731
A family adventure park with a fun
fair, theatre, play barn, exotic animals,
restaurant and coffee shop.
Oakwood Theme Park
Narberth. Roller coasters and more.
Tel: 01834 891376;
www.oakwoodthemepark.co.uk
Teifi Valley Narrow Gauge Railway
Nr Newcastle Emlyn.
Tel: 01559 371077;
www.teifivalleyrailway.com

SHOPPING
Market Days
Fishguard, Thu. Farmers' market
fortnightly, Sat.
Haverfordwest fortnightly, Fri.
Pembroke Dock fortnightly, Sat.
St David's, Women's Institute, Thu.
Tenby, indoors, Mon, Tue, Thu–Sat.

PERFORMING ARTS
Fishguard
Theatr Gwaun.
Milford Haven
Torch Theatre.
Narberth
Queens Hall.

SPORTS & ACTIVITIES
ANGLING
Boat Fishing
Short trips or day-long deep-sea
fishing trips from many harbours.
Tenby: Tel: 07974 623542;
www.tenbyfishing.co.uk
Solva: Tel: 01437 720053;
www.solva.net
Neyland: 01646 600313;
www.celticwildcat.com

Coarse Fishing

Yet-y-Gors Fishery, Manorwen,
Fishguard Tel:01348 873497;
www.yet-y-gors.co.uk
Two coarse lakes plus still-water
fly-fishing for trout.
Holgan Farm, Narberth.
Tel: 07796 517586;
www.fisheries.co.uk
Carp and tench lakes.

BEACHES

Among the best beaches for
sunbathing and swimming are
those at Barrafundle (Stackpole),
Broadhaven, Marloes, Saundersfoot,
Tenby, Newport and Whitesands Bay
(St David's). Always take note of safety
instructions. Watersports enthusiasts
head for Broadhaven, Freshwater West,
Manorbier and St Brides Bay.

BOAT TRIPS

Tenby to Caldey Island

Leave from Tenby. Tel: 01834 844453;
www.caldey-island.co.uk

Neyland/Martin's Haven to Grassholm, Skokholm and Skomer

Tel: 01646 603110;
www.dale-sailing.co.uk

St David's to Ramsey Island

Wildlife trips to and around Ramsey.
www.ramseyisland.co.uk
www.thousandislands.co.uk
www.aquaphobia-ramseyisland.co.uk

Cardigan Bay

Cetacean watching and trips
from the Teifi Estuary.
Tel: 01239 623558
www.baytoremember.co.uk

CYCLING

Old railways, reservoir roads, byways,
coastal and hill tracks. For general info
visit www.cyclepembrokeshire.com

Bike hire

Newport.
Tel: 01239 820773;
www.newportbikehire.com;
Haverfordwest.
Tel: 01437 760068;
www.mikes-bikes.co.uk
Fishguard.
Tel: 01348 874170;
www.pembrokeshirebikes.co.uk

HORSE RIDING
Dunes Riding Centre
Cotts Lane, Martlewy, Narberth.
Tel: 01834 891398;
www.dunes-riding.co.uk
East Nolton Riding Stables
East Nolton Farm, Nolton Haven,
Haverfordwest.
Tel: 01437 710360;
www.noltonstables.com
Havard Stables
Trewyddig Fawr, Dinas Cross, Newport.
Tel: 01348 811452
Llanwnda Riding & Trekking
Penrhiw Fach, Llanwnda, Goodwick.
Tel: 01348 873595

WALKING
Pembrokeshire Coast Path National
Trail: for information about walking
this long distance path and hundreds of
other walking routes visit the National
Park website.
www.pcnpa.org.uk
Year-round coastal bus services for
walkers (buses run on chip fat).
Tel: 01437 764551
www.pembrokeshire.gov.uk/coastbus

WATER SPORTS
Coasteering
St David's. Tel: 01437 721611;
www.tyf.com
Kitesurfing
Newgale Beach. Tel: 07816 169359;
www.bigbluekitesurfing.com
Sea Kayaking
County-wide. Tel: 01348 837709;
www.preseliadventure.co.uk
Surfing
Newgale, Manorbier, Freshwater West.
Tel: 01646 680070;
www.outerreefsurfschool.co.uk

EVENTS & CUSTOMS
Fishguard
Folk Festival, May.
International Music Festival, Jun.
Jazz festival Sep.
Narberth
Winter carnival, early Dec.
Newport/Preseli
Walking Festival, May.
St David's
Cathedral festival May/Jun.
Tenby
Arts festival late Sep.

The Boathouse Tea Room
Stable Yard, Stackpole
SA71 5DE
Tel: 01646 672672
Close to the old stone jetty, this popular licensed café has a large outdoor area for alfresco dining. The quiches are delicious, while tasty sandwiches include fresh crab and cream teas have tempting cakes.

Morawelon Café Bar & Restaurant
Parrog, Newport, Pembrokeshire
SA42 0RW
Tel: 01239 820565
Set on the Parrog beachfront, you can indulge yourself here with many varieties of tea or coffee and delicious cakes, or you can tuck into a mouth-watering meal that might include freshly caught local crab, washed down with a cool glass of white wine.

The Old Printing House
20 Main Street, Solva
SA62 6UU
Tel: 01437 721603
The award-winning tea room/restaurant is located at the heart of the village in an 18th-century house and paper mill with beamed ceilings and stripped stone walls. The tea room is noted for its freshly baked bread and cakes, home-made chutneys and cream teas.

Tudor Lodge Restaurant
Jameston, Manorbier
SA70 7SS
Tel: 01834 871978
www.tudorlodgerestaurant.co.uk
This restaurant has a clean, modern style. Walls are hung with contemporary paintings, there is a good atmosphere and traditional, blazing log fires. The food is excellent and prepared using fresh local produce wherever possible, whether it is for light lunches or evening meals.

LOWER FISHGUARD

Cambrian Inn
6, Main Street, Solva
SA62 6UU
Tel: 01437 721210
www.cambrianinn.co.uk
The 16th-century inn sited at the
entrance to Lower Solva offers
restaurant and bar meals in
comfortable cosy surroundings.
Expect fresh pasta, steaks and
vegetarian dishes with real ales
such as Brains Reverend James
or Wye Valley Butty Bach.

St Brides Inn
St Brides Road, Little Haven
SA62 3UN
Tel: 01437 781266
www.stbridesinn.co.uk
This charming little inn has wooden
pews inside a compact dining area,
with stripped stone walls and an
ancient well in one corner. Good food
is served here with a daily specials
board that often includes locally caught
seafood. There's also a beer garden,
where meals and barbecues are served
throughout the summer.

The Stackpole Inn
Jasons Corner, Stackpole SA71 5DF
Tel: 01646 672324
www.stackpoleinn.co.uk
The 17th-century Stackpole Inn is
popular with walkers and locals.
The award-winning bar and restaurant
menu includes fresh locally caught
fish that appear on the 'just in' specials
board and old favourites such as Welsh
Black beef.

Tafarn Sinc
Rosebush SA66 7QT
Tel: 01437 532214
www.tafarnsinc.co.uk
This red-painted corrugated building
that used to be a railway halt promises
little on first sight and when you
realise that there's sawdust on the
floor you might be put off. But this
Welsh-speaking, friendly pub has been
likened to a museum of local history
inside, with old photos and curios on
every wall. The pub has its own-brewed
beer, Cwrw Tafarn Sinc, and serves
delicious food including the most
succulent steaks.

WORMS HEAD

Gower Peninsula & Coast

INTRODUCTION

The limestone cliffs and golden sandy bays of the Gower Peninsula have been protected from unsympathetic development – industrial and residential – since it was designated as Britain's first Area of Outstanding Natural Beauty in 1956. Further east, Cardiff is in every sense the capital of Wales. It has a rich industrial, commercial and cultural heritage, but has evolved into a modern, vibrant and cosmopolitan city. Cardiff Bay is now fringed with restaurants, bars and shops. Among its many attractions are Techniquest, Butetown History and Arts Centre, and a superb Millennium Centre.

NASH POINT

ESSENTIAL SIGHTS

Unmissable attractions

Enjoy shopping, good food, culture and a host of other treats in Cardiff... explore historic Monmouth, the birthplace of Henry V...go in search of Dylan Thomas at Laugharne...explore the Gower Peninsula and discover superb Rhossili Bay and coast...meander around two castles at Grosmont and Skenfrith on a quiet cycle ride.

2

1 **Rhossili**
Rhossili Bay is one of the finest stretches of flat sands in Wales.

2 **Cardiff**
Cardiff's Millennium Stadium, in the heart of the city, hosts major sporting events and concerts.

215

CARDIFF

Today the capital of Wales is the pride of the principality, a flourishing modern city, but one that hasn't forgotten its roots. Its history goes back 2,000 years to the time of the Romans and it's all encompassed within the walls of Cardiff Castle which stands proudly, right in the centre of the city. The moated Norman castle, whose 12th-century keep has survived, was built on the site of the Roman fort – some of the Roman foundation walls can still be seen. Like many Welsh castles, Cardiff was left ruinous by Owain Glyndwr but it was rebuilt by Richard Beauchamp, the Earl of Warwick, and continued to serve as a residence for several centuries.

Cardiff's prosperity, and gradual rise to importance, came with the Industrial Revolution. The discovery of coking coal allowed the iron-smelting industry to flourish in the valleys to the north and Cardiff became the obvious choice as a port. At this time the wealthy Bute family, who were descendants of the royal Stuarts, moved here. They enlarged the docks and made Cardiff into one of the world's largest coal and iron exporting ports and they also took possession of Cardiff Castle. The 3rd Marquis of Bute commissioned William Burges to redevelop the living quarters into the Gothic Victorian style you see today. No expense was spared: the interiors were opulent, using marble, gold leaf and fine hardwoods from around the world. Many of the rooms have amazing decorated ceilings, stained-glass windows, murals of historical and mythological figures, and fine works of art on the walls. The ornate clock tower looks over the city, as Big Ben does in London.

The city centre buildings are a mix of modern, Victorian and Edwardian, with shopping arcades criss-crossing the main streets. The classic Portland stone buildings of the Law Courts, City Hall and the National Museum present an impressive front to the Civic Centre

Visit

CASTELL COCH – THE RED CASTLE

This fairy-tale castle, a few miles north of Cardiff, echoes those in Bavaria with its circular red sandstone towers and conical roofs. Built on a limestone outcrop on wooded hill-slopes, the original Norman castle had fallen into disrepair, but the 3rd Marquis of Bute commissioned William Burges to refurbish it to the same extravagant standards that he exercised on Cardiff Castle.

and university areas, while the open spaces of Bute Park behind the castle take you to the banks of the River Taff. Here you can catch a waterbus past the famous Cardiff Arms Park and the much larger Millennium Stadium to Cardiff Bay, where the old dockyards, which declined with the end of the Welsh coalfield, have been transformed into a busy, thriving waterfront. The controversial Cardiff Bay Barrage construction has created a massive freshwater lake out of the bay, but still allows the fish to pass through.

On the waterfront the famous terracotta Pierhead Building is joined by two revolutionary buildings: the Senedd Building, which houses the National Assembly of Wales, and the Millennium Centre, which presents the performing arts. The latter, built from local slate, has a bilingual inscription in very large lettering: 'In these stones horizons sing', which says a lot about 21st-century Cardiff.

LAUGHARNE & WEST CARMARTHEN COASTLINE

Lying on the western bank of the Taf, Laugharne, which is pronounced Larn, is dominated by the imposing shell of its Norman castle. The castle is perched on a tree-cloaked cliff looking out across the salt marshes and creeks of the estuary and was immortalised by J M W Turner. The main street, lined with Georgian houses, antiquarian shops and bistros, leads to the unusual

LAUGHARNE CASTLE

CHEPSTOW CASTLE

whitewashed town hall, which has a modest clock tower. Laugharne and Malmesbury in Wiltshire are the only two United Kingdom towns to have retained a charter granted by Royal Decree. The charter, kept in the town hall, allows the people to be governed by a corporation in addition to other tiers of government.

Laugharne is synonymous with Dylan Thomas, the Welsh poet and author of *Under Milk Wood*, who lived here off and on for many years. Thomas spent the last four years of his life (1949–53) at the Boathouse. This romantically situated cottage overlooking the estuary is now a museum dedicated to his life and works. Visitors can also view his writing shed, sited on a terrace above the house.

Travelling on to Carmarthen Bay the road from Laugharne comes to Pendine, whose firm beach of sands and shells stretches for 7 miles (11km) between Gilman Point and Laugharne Sands. In the early 20th century the beach was considered ideal for world land speed records, including Malcolm Campbell's 146.16mph (235.22kmph) record in 1924. These ended with the fatal accident of Parry Thomas-Jones, whose car, Babs, rolled over in the 1927 attempt for the world land speed record. Babs can be seen in Pendine's Museum of Speed. Note: The beach is owned by the MoD and they do occasionally restrict public access in the area.

MONMOUTH & WYE VALLEY

Historic Monmouth stands at the confluence of the rivers Wye and Monnow. It was the birthplace of Henry V, whose statue stands in Agincourt Square looking down upon a statue of another of the town's favourite sons, Charles Rolls, aviation pioneer and co-founder of Rolls-Royce. Its 13th-century bridge over the River Monnow is the only surviving medieval one in Britain to have included a fortified gatehouse, which at one time would have had a portcullis and sentry rampart.

The town is a good base for an exploration of the Wye Valley and its lovely riverside walks. Just a few miles south lies Tintern Abbey, founded by the Cistercian order in the 12th century. Despite being roofless, the abbey's graceful arches of the Decorated style and great windows remain almost complete, embellished by their exquisite surroundings in the wooded valley.

Chepstow, near the mouth of the Wye, is known for its massive Norman castle, which stands on formidable cliffs high above the river. It's best viewed from the east bank.

PARKMILL

Parkmill shelters in the shady sylvan bowers of Ilston Cwm, a limestone valley that winds its way from inland Gower to the coast at Three Cliff Bay. Centred around the only working mill on the peninsula the village is popular with both tourists who come to see the Gower Heritage Centre, with its craft workshops and museum, and walkers.

Visit

KIDWELLY CASTLE

Built on a steep grassy mound looking down on the River Gwendraeth, Kidwelly is one of the best-preserved castles in South Wales. The old timber castle built by the Normans in the early 12th century was destroyed in a heavy attack by Llywelyn the Great in 1231, but was rebuilt in the 1270s. Unusually, the superb gatehouse forms part of the outer walls. It is now managed by CADW.

To the northwest you can take a stroll through the woods of Green Cwm to visit the Giant's Grave, a megalithic tomb dating back to 3500 BC, or head southwards down Ilston Cwm. This route leads through more woodland before continuing beneath the huge dunes of Pennard Burrows, on top of which lie the impressive ruins of Pennard Castle and its church, with their sheer drop below. The 13th-century castle was established by the Norman invaders.

225

Visit

OXWICH NATIONAL NATURE RESERVE

As an area of Outstanding Natural Beauty, Oxwich Bay combines wildlife with all the appeal of a superb beach resort. It is an excellent location for swimming, surfing and nature appreciation. The beach is easily accessible and the reserve supports several diverse wildlife habitats, including freshwater lakes and marshes, swamps, salt marshes, dunes, cliffs and woodland. The freshwater marsh was artificially created when Sir Thomas Mansel Talbot of Penrice Estate built a wall to prevent encroachment from the sea. The reserve has more than 600 species of flowering plants. You are likely to see ringed plovers, curlews, oystercatchers and gulls feeding on the wet sands at low tide, along with wigeons and warblers on the marshes.

However, it appears in few historical records and has always been dogged by sand encroachment. To this day, known remnants remain buried in the sands for their own preservation.

A lazy stream meanders and trickles into the beautiful golden sands of Three Cliff Bay beneath the stunning, almost vertical limestone strata of the Three Cliffs. The popular climbers' crags begin a fine stretch of superb cliff scenery past the houses of Southgate to Pwlldu Head. Pwlldu means Blackpool, but that's where the similarity ends, for you'll find yourself looking down from this massive headland to a pebble storm beach at the head of the lovely wooded limestone gorge of the Bishopston Valley.

Surfers love the commercialised Caswell Bay, a sandy cove overlooked by pines and self-catering apartments. At Mumbles the world of Gower has collided with that of urban Swansea. A pier, amusement parlours, ice cream kiosks and cafés make country lovers feel they want to retreat rather quickly back to real Gower, although it is a great playground for the children who may wish to stay, play and eat.

THE GLORY OF GOD
AND IN MEMORY OF
WILLIAM (BILLY) GIBBS, COXSWAIN
WILLIAM EYNON, SECOND COXSWAIN
GEORGE HARRY, LIFEBOATMAN
WHO WERE DROWNED OFF FULL...
ON 1ST JANUARY 1916 WHEN THE PORT EINON
'JANET' WAS CAPSIZED WHI...
ENDEAVOURING TO RENDER ASSISTANCE...

PORT EINON

After threading through the outskirts of Swansea, the wide-open spaces of Fairwood Common and flirting with the coast at Pennard, Gower's only major road, the A4118 ends at little Port Einon on the southwest coast. The last stretch through the village is narrow, rarely wide enough for two cars to pass. The village is a mix of Gower's rugged coastline and small-scale commercialism.

Dunes and cobbles line a sandy beach, all then surrounded by rugged cliffs dotted with the typical Gower lime-washed cottages. There's a real old-fashioned seaside atmosphere, with beachwear and bucket and spade shops, a couple of fish and chip shop cafés and a surf shop. However, the visitor is only a short walk away from rugged cliffs and secluded rocky coves. The coast walk to Worms Head and Rhossili is the finest in Gower.

Port Einon gets its name from the 11th-century Welsh prince, Einon ap Owain and it is believed that he built the long-gone Port Einon. The village's history is inextricably linked to the sea. In its heyday of the 19th-century more than 40 oyster skiffs operated from the port and limestone from a nearby quarry was exported. The blue-green stones you'll see scattered on the shoreline are not part of Gower geology but ballast from the cargo ships.

Tales of smuggling are common and it is said that the old salt house, the ruin beneath the cliffs of the western promontory, was used by the Lucas family as a storehouse for contraband. At one time there were eight customs and excise officers based here. Next to the salt house is the youth hostel. The building was formerly a lifeboat station but this was closed following a rescue attempt that went dreadfully wrong. Called out during a winter storm of 1916 the volunteer crew were caught out by horrendous waves, which capsized the boat twice, drowning three of the crew. A monument has been erected in the churchyard as

231

RHOSSILI BEACH

a tribute to their bravery. Oxwich Point separates Port Einon Bay from the larger sandy sweep of Oxwich Bay, an ideal location for swimming and surfing and also appealing to nature lovers who can visit the nature reserve. The ruins of Sir Rice Mansel's magnificent Tudor mansion, known as Oxwich Castle are perched on the headland overlooking the bay. It is now managed by CADW.

RHOSSILI

At the western end of the peninsula facing Carmarthen Bay, Rhossili is the pride of Gower: a perfect, gently arcing sandy beach flanked by the 250-foot (76m) high sandstone cliffs and steep grassy banks of Rhossili Down. Each day high tide makes islands out of the tiny outcrop of Burry Holms in the north and the mile (1.6km) long rocky spit of Worms Head in the south.

On many days at Rhossili the breeze will be up and the bay will then attracts all sorts of surfers.

Visit

THE GOWER HERITAGE CENTRE

Themed around a 12th-century water-powered corn mill built by the Norman baron, William de Breos, the Gower Heritage Centre opened in 1990 as a countryside crafts centre. It is open to visitors who can explore the sawmill, wheelwright's shop, miller's cottage, agricultural museum, craft shop and tea room. There's a children's play area and numerous small animals, including chickens and ducks, and recently housed exhibits from the former Maritime Museum in Swansea.

Activity

WORMS HEAD

The string of islets that thrust defiantly into the Atlantic at the bay's southernmost tip is known as Worms Head. It is now a nature reserve, but can be reached at low tide by scrambling across the rocky causeway at the western tip of the promontory. It's essential that you check the tide timetables before making a sortie.

GOWER PENINSULA & COAST

When the tide is out you'll see the wooden skeleton of the coaster, *Helvetia*, driven ashore by the gales of 1887. Rhossili Down at 632 feet (193m) is the highest place on Gower; there's a splendid bridleway straddling its heights. On the summit are the Sweyne's Howes burial chambers.

Rhossili village has one large hotel and a National Trust information centre and shop. A large car park gives access to the long beach and to Worms Head. Tides are of the utmost importance for those wanting to scramble across the rocky causeway to the headland: consult the timetables posted on the National Trust shop and the coastguard's station.

SWANSEA

Little is recorded of Swansea until the Norman conquerors saw its potential as a port. In 1106 Henry de Beaumont, 1st Earl of Warwick, built a motte and bailey castle on a cliff overlooking the mouth of the Tawe. After the Welsh sacked the castle in the 13th century, the old structure was rebuilt. The current building dates back to the 14th century, though it didn't have much of a strategic role following the defeat of the Welsh by Edward I. In 1306 Swansea was given the Royal Charter to build and repair ships, a tradition going into the 20th century.

During the 19th century large-scale anthracite mining and the metal industry changed this small village into the metropolis it is today. By the 1850s the railways had arrived, the first dockyard had been completed and Swansea was supplying 60 per cent of the world's copper requirements. Swansea's other face was that of a seaside resort – railway adverts compared Swansea Bay with the Bay of Naples and well-to-do Victorians came to take the sea air. Second World War bombing by the German *Luftwaffe* and the mid-20th-century decline in manufacturing saw the city having to reinvent itself.

SWANSEA

SWANSEA MARINA

Still a little down-at-heel in the suburbs, Swansea has become a vibrant city, full of culture and new ideas. The dock area has been redeveloped into an opulent Maritime Quarter, where refurbished old buildings share streets with modern architecture such as the National Waterfront Museum, and where you can see vivid reminders of the city's industrial and maritime past. Take a stroll around the 600-berth yachting marina and over the elegant Sail Bridge across the Tawe – which is not only a landmark in itself but also provides sightseers with cycle and pedestrian access – then pop in to see the exhibition at the Dylan Thomas Centre.

A fine shopping centre surrounds the castle. Music lovers can see international artists at Brangwyn Hall or operas at the Grand Theatre. The Glynn Vivian Art Gallery, which has a fine collection of paintings and sculpture from old masters and modern artists, also has displays of Swansea porcelain.

DYLAN THOMAS STATUE, SWANSEA

TOURIST INFORMATION CENTRES

Caerleon
5 High Street.
Tel: 01633 422656

Cardiff Visitor Centre
The Old Library, The Hayes.
Tel: 02920 873573;
www.visitcardiff.com

Chepstow
Castle Car Park, Bridge Street.
Tel: 01291 623772

Mumbles
522 Mumbles Road.
Tel: 01792 361302

Monmouth
Priory Street.
Tel: 01600 713899;
www.visitwyevalley.com

Swansea
Plymouth Street.
Tel: 01792 468321;
www.visitswanseabay.com

PLACES OF INTEREST

The Big Pit: National Coal Museum
Blaenavon.
Tel: 01496 790311;
www.museumwales.ac.uk
Free.

The Boat House
Dylan's Walk, Laugharne.
Tel: 01994 427420;
www.dylanthomasboathouse.com

Caerleon
www.caerleon.net
Roman fort. Free.

Caerphilly Castle
Tel: 02920 883143;
www.caerphillycastle.com

Cardiff Castle
Tel: 02920 878100;
www.cardiffcastle.com

Castell Coch
Tel: 02920 810101

Dylan Thomas Centre
Somerset Place, Swansea.
Tel: 01792 463980

Gower Heritage Centre
Parkmill, Gower.
Tel: 01792 371206;
www.gowerheritagecentre.co.uk

Llandaff Cathedral
Free.

Llanerch Vineyard
Hensol, Pendoylan, Vale of Glamorgan.
Tel: 01443 225877;
www. llanerch-vineyard.co.uk
Free.

Museum of Speed
Pendine.
Tel: 01994 453488
Interpretation of the use of the
sands at Pendine for land speed
attempts and racing. Free.

The National Botanic Garden of Wales
Llanarthne.
Tel: 01558 668768;
www.gardenofwales.org.uk

National Museum
Cathays Park, Cardiff.
Tel: 02920 397951;
www.museumwales.ac.uk Free.

National Waterfront Museum
Oystermouth Road, Swansea.
Tel: 01792 638950;
www.museumwales.ac.uk
Tells the story of the industrialisation
of Wales with exhibits, including
working engines. Free.

**National Wetland
Centre Wales**
Burry Inlet, Llanelli.
Tel: 01554 7410877;
www.wwt.org.uk/llanelli

Raglan Castle
Tel: 01291 690228
Off A40 between Monmouth and
Abergavenny.

Rhondda Heritage Park
Lewis Merthyr Colliery, Trehafod.
Tel: 01443 682036;
www.rhonddaheritagepark.com

Tintern Abbey
Wye Valley.
Tel: 01291 689251

FOR CHILDREN

Pembrey Country Park
Burry Port.
Tel: 01554 833913 (Parks Manager).
Seaside park with crazy golf, dry
ski slope, toboggan run and a
miniature railway.

GOWER PENINSULA & COAST

PERFORMING ARTS
Blake Theatre
Monmouth. Tel: 01600 719401
Brangwyn Hall
Swansea. Tel: 01792 635432
Chapter Arts Centre
Cardiff. Tel: 029 20 311050
Grand Theatre
Swansea. Tel: 01792 475715
Millennium Centre
Cardiff. Tel: 02920 636464
St David's Hall
Cardiff. Tel: 02920 878444
Savoy Theatre
Monmouth. Tel: 01600 772467

SPORTS & ACTIVITIES
BEACHES
Barry Island
Two excellent beaches for bathers.
Carmarthenshire
Cefn Sidan, Pembrey Sands.
Eight miles (13km) of fine sands and
dunes via Pembrey Country Park near
Burry Port. Lifeguards here in summer.
Caswell Bay
Excellent small beach, popular with
surfers. Good café. No dogs May–Sep.

Glamorgan Heritage Coast
Porthcawl.
The town's four beaches here are
popular for bathing and watersports.
Oxwich Bay
Sand dunes overlook Gower's second
largest beach. Good for bathing,
canoeing and sailing, some surfing.
Pendine Sands
An 'endless' beach that once facilitated
land speed record attempts.
Port Einon Bay
Commercialised beach with cafés,
campsites and gift shops.
No dogs May–Sep.
Rhossili Bay
Huge crescent-shaped sandy cove,
popular with surfers and hang-gliders.
BOAT TRIPS
Gower Coast
Speedboat trips in a rigid inflatable.
Tel: 07866 250440;
www.gowercoastadventures.co.uk
Bay Island Voyages
Lock Keeper's Cottage, Britannia Park
Cardiff. Cruises around Cardiff Bay and
the coast. Tel: 01446 420692;
www.bayisland.co.uk

CYCLING

Sustrans trails include: Cardiff: Taff
Trail to Brecon Beacons; Llanelli:
Swiss Valley & Millennium Coastal
Park; Monmouth: Peregrine Path.

CYCLE HIRE

Abergavenny

Pedalaway. Tel: 01873 830219;
www.pedalaway.co.uk

Cardiff Bay

Pedal Power. Tel: 07775 616411;
www.cardiffpedalpower.org

Llanelli

Merlin Cycle Tours. Tel: 01554 756603;
www.merlincycletours.co.uk

Monmouth

Pedalabikeaway
Tel: 01600 772821;
www.pedalabikeaway.co.uk

HORSE RIDING

Llanthony Riding and Trekking

Court Farm, Llanthony.
Tel: 01873 890359;
www.llanthony.co.uk

Marros Riding Centre

Marros, Pendine.
Tel: 01994 453238;
www.marros-farm.co.uk

Parc-Le-Breos Riding Centre

Penmaen, Gower. Tel: 01792 371636;
www.parc-le-breos.co.uk

SURFING

Rhossili

Sam's Surf Shack
Rhossili, Gower SA3 1PL
Tel: 01792 390519;
www.samssurfshack.com

EVENTS & CUSTOMS

Cardiff

Cardiff Summer Festival, Jul–Aug.

Chepstow

Agricultural Show, mid-Aug.

Crickhowell

Crickhowell Walking Festival, Mar.
Tel: 01873 811970;
www.crickhowellfestival.com

Gower

Gower Walking Festival, mid-Jun.
Tel: 01792 361302;
www.visitmumbles.co.uk

Monmouth

Monmouth Show, end Aug.

Swansea

Swansea Festival of Music and Arts.
Celebration of arts, entertainment, Oct.

TEA ROOMS

The Bay Bistro & Coffee House
Rhossili, Gower SA3 1PL
Tel: 01792 390519
Enjoy magnificent views across the bay while enjoying hot chocolate, a laverbread burger or a baked Camembert; great cream teas and cakes too! Evening meals include the freshest local fish.

Norwegian Church
Harbour Drive, Cardiff Bay,
Cardiff CF10 4PA
Tel: 02920 877959
Built in 1869 as a place of worship for the large number of Scandinavian sailors in Cardiff, the white wooden building has a popular tea room where you can indulge yourself with excellent cakes and a range of snacks.

Part y Seal
Grosmont, Monmouthshire NP7 8LE
Tel: 01981 240814
Here you can enjoy a relaxing morning coffee, lunch or afternoon tea in a splendid rural setting. The old stone cottage has delightful gardens for alfresco summer dining or glowing fires for the short winter days. The produce is home grown and organic. There's also an Oriental giftware shop and Fairytaleland with its seasonally changing scenes.

Café at the National Waterfront Museum
Oystermouth Road, Maritime Quarter,
Swansea SA1 3RD
Tel: 01792 638950
At the heart of the ultra-modern museum buildings in Swansea's Maritime Quarter, the café offers a good choice of excellent cakes, sandwiches, quiches, various savouries and appetising hot meals. Everything is made on-site using fresh produce sourced locally wherever possible.

Abbey Hotel

Llanthony Priory, Llanthony,
Monmouthshire NP7 7NN
Tel: 01873 890487

Many pubs are next door to a church, but this one is in the grounds of the Cistercian priory. Serves lunches and evening meals (also ice creams and hot drinks). Refreshments under the cloisters – what a setting!

Bell at Skenfrith

Skenfrith, Monmouthshire NP7 8UH
Tel: 01600 750235

Splendidly sited by the bridge at Skenfrith, this luxurious 17th-century coaching inn serves fine cuisine sourced 'from as many local farms and suppliers as possible'. Main courses might include fillet of Brecon beef or glazed breast of local duck. The food is complemented by a good wine list and real ales, including Wye Valley and Kingstone, and Ty Gwyn local scrumpy.

Castle View Hotel

Bridge Street, Chepstow NP16 5EZ
Tel: 01291 620349
www.hotelchepstow.co.uk

A 300-year-old, ivy-clad, whitewashed pub looking across to the castle and the River Wye. Superb cuisine showcases British specialities with local produce including steaks, and salmon caught from the Wye. There's a charming small beer garden.

King Arthur Hotel

Higher Green, Reynoldston,
Gower SA3 1AD
Tel: 01792 390775
www.kingarthurhotel.co.uk

Set back from the large village green, the King Arthur Hotel is well known for its local Welsh dishes including game, steaks, pork, laverbread and locally caught fish and cockles. There's a cosy atmosphere with log fires and for summer there's a pleasant garden.

USEFUL INFORMATION

USEFUL NUMBERS

Brecon Beacons National Park Visitors/Mountain Centre
Libanus, Brecon, Powys.
Tel: 01874 623366

The Gower Society
Swansea Museum,
Victoria Road, Swansea.
www.gowersociety.welshnet.co.uk

Pembrokeshire Coast National Park Centre
Oriel y Parc, St David's.
Tel: 01437 720392;
www.orielyparc.co.uk

Snowdonia National Park Authority
Penrhyndeudraeth,
Gwynedd.
Tel: 01766 770274;
www.eryri-npa.gov.uk

Visit Wales Centre
Tel: 08708 300306;
www.visitwales.co.uk

ANCIENT MONUMENTS

Most castles, abbeys and ruins in Wales are managed by CADW.

CADW
Plas Carew, Unit 5/7 Cefn Coed,
Parc Nantgarw,
Cardiff CF15 7QQ
Tel: 01443 336000;
www.cadw.wales.gov.uk

ANGLING

Visit Wales publish a free brochure with a list of tackle shops and places to fish, available from TICs or from www.fishing.visitwales.com

CYCLING

Visit Wales publish a free brochure, available from TICs or their website www.cycling.visitwales.com
A National cycle network, including a trans-Wales route from Chepstow to Holyhead, Lon Las Cymru, is operated by Sustrans National Cycle Network.
Tel: 0117 926 8893;
www.sustrans.org.uk

WALKING

Visit Wales
www.walking.visitwales.com

NATIONAL LONG DISTANCE PATHS

The Cambrian Way

A 275-mile (444km) route over
the Brecon Beacons,
Mid Wales and Snowdonia.

Offa's Dyke Path

A 170-mile (274km) route
from Chepstow to Prestatyn.

Glyndwr's Way

A 132-mile (212km) route
through Mid-Wales.

Pembrokeshire Coast Path

A 186-mile (300km) coastal route
from Tenby to St Dogmaels.

VISITORS WITH DISABILITIES

Disabilities Wales
Tel: 02920 887325;
www.disabilitywales.org

INDEX

ACKNOWLEDGEMENTS

The Automobile Association would like to thank the following photographers, companies and picture libraries for their assistance in the preparation of this book.

Abbreviations for the picture credits are as follows – (t) top; (b) bottom; (c) centre; (l) left; (r) right; (AA) AA World Travel Library.

2/3 AA; 5 AA/G Matthews; 6 AA/N Jenkins; 9 AA/N Jenkins; 12/13 AA/R Eames; 14 AA/C&A Molyneux; 15t AA/P Aithie; 15b AA/S Watkins; 16l AA/G Matthews; 16r AA/N Jenkins; 17t AA/G Matthews; 17b AA/G Matthews; 19 AA/I Burgum; 20 AA/N Jenkins; 23 AA/I Burgum; 24 AA; 26 AA/P Aithie; 28/29 AA/I Burgum; 30 AA/G Matthews; 31 AA/N Jenkins; 32 AA/I Burgum; 33 AA/P Aithie; 34 AA; 37 AA/S Watkins; 38/39 AA/N Jenkins; 43 AA/S Watkins; 44 AA/A Grierley; 47 AA/G Matthews; 48 AA/P Aithie; 55 AA/G Munday; 56 AA/D Croucher; 58 AA/S Watkins; 60/61 AA/S Watkins; 62 AA/S Watkins; 63 AA/N Jenkins; 64t AA/D Croucher; 64b AA/N Jenkins; 65l AA/R Newton; 65r AA/N Jenkins; 66 AA/R Newton; 70 AA/R Eames; 73 AA/S Watkins; 74 AA/R Newton; 77 AA/R Newton; 78/79 AA/N Jenkins; 82 AA/R Eames; 85 AA/M Bauer; 86/87 AA/H Williams; 89 AA/S Lewis; 90/91 AA/S Watkins; 92 AA/G Matthews; 99 AA/S Watkins; 100 AA/G Matthews; 102 AA/N Jenkins; 104/105 AA/I Burgum; 106 AA/R Newton; 107t AA/N Jenkins; 107b AA/C Jones; 108/109 AA/G Matthews; 109 AA/D Croucher; 110 AA/D Croucher; 113 AA/N Jenkins; 114/115 AA/I Burgum; 117 AA/I Burgum; 119 AA/R Newton; 120/121 AA/C Jones; 122/123 AA/I Burgum; 124 AA/N Jenkins; 126 AA/N Jenkins; 135 AA/C Jones; 136 AA/I Burgum; 138 AA/I Burgum; 140/141 AA/N Jenkins; 142 AA/I Burgum; 143 AA/C Molyneux; 144t AA/D Croucher; 144b AA/R Eames; 145 AA/C&A Molyneux; 146/147 AA/N Jenkins; 150/151 AA/N Jenkins; 153 AA/N Jenkins; 154 AA/H Williams; 156 AA/N Jenkins; 159 AA/C Molyneux; 162/163 AA/C&A Molyneux; 165 AA/C Molyneux; 171 AA/D Santillo; 172 AA/N Jenkins; 174 AA/R Ireland; 176/177 AA/M Moody; 178 AA/M Allwood-Coppin; 179t AA/N Jenkins; 179b AA/C Molyneux; 180 AA/C Molyneux; 181 AA/I Burgum; 182 AA/C Molyneux; 186 AA/N Jenkins; 189 AA/I Burgum; 190/191 AA/N Jenkins; 195 AA/N Jenkins; 196 AA/M Moody; 198/199 AA/M Moody; 201 AA/N Jenkins; 207 AA/M Moody; 208 AA/N Jenkins; 210 AA; 212/213 AA/H Williams; 214 AA/N Jenkins; 215 AA/N Jenkins; 216t AA/I Burgum; 216b AA/I Burgum; 217 AA/N Jenkins; 219 AA/N Jenkins; 221 AA; 222 AA/H Williams; 224 AA/N Jenkins; 226/227 AA/N Jenkins; 229 AA/H Williams; 230 AA/I Burgum; 232 AA/N Jenkins; 234/235 AA/M Moody; 237 AA/C Jones; 238/239 AA; 240/241 AA/I Burgum; 247 AA/I Burgum; 249 AA/N Jenkins.

Every effort has been made to trace the copyright holders, and we apologise in advance for any unintentional omissions or errors. We would be pleased to apply any corrections in a following edition of this publication.